RECORDED VERSIONS GUITAR ®

AUTHENTIC TRANSCRIPTIONS
WITH NOTES AND TABLATURE

**Transcribed by
HEMME LUTTJEBOER
and KERRY O'BRIEN**

QUEEN

MW00564516

GREATEST HITS

ISBN 978-0-7935-3850-8

**HAL•LEONARD®
CORPORATION**

7777 W. BLUEMOUND RD. P.O. BOX 13819 MILWAUKEE, WI 53213

THE CROWN JEWELS
QUEEN
GREATEST HITS

by Mike Mettler

When you think of Queen, you've gotta think *big*. Grandiose. Extravagant. Over the top, but never out of bounds. Their incredible reign lasted from early 1973 until frontman Freddie Mercury's untimely death in late 1991, but they haven't handed over the crown entirely just yet. Guitar wizards like Nuno Bettencourt and Slash continue to sing the praises of Queen and especially the band's lanky guitarist, Brian May, whose patented harmonic crunch guided the band to international superstardom with gripping, incendiary tracks like "Killer Queen," "Bohemian Rhapsody," "We Will Rock You," and "Crazy Little Thing Called Love." Building on his own love for the styles of skiffle, rockabilly and instrumental surf rock, as well as the prowess of noted British guitar giants like Beck, Clapton and Page (all of whom he saw play live in their '60s heydays), May deftly straddled the line between progressive rock and glam rock to concoct the patented layered and textured Queen sound.

Queen's legacy is a singular one, one that defies labels; Queen is simply Queen. They are the bridge that leads from Yes to Boston and from Led Zeppelin to Guns N' Roses. Combining a keen pop sensibility with a bit of metallic crunch and a flair for the theatrical, Queen turned their songs into full-blown, multi-faceted narratives that would do William Shakespeare proud.

Photo by Chris Walter/RETNA LTD.

But the road to the throne at the top of the rock-and-roll hierarchy was not an easy one for May and company. In fact, it was a long, arduous trip. The guitarist, born July 19, 1947, held a degree in physics and math from London's Imperial College, and had aspirations of becoming a teacher if his rock career didn't take off, taking care to also pursue a graduate degree in astronomy.

Photo by David Wainwright/RETNA LTD.

May's fertile creative mind was always on the go. He couldn't afford to buy the Stratocaster he so badly wanted when he turned 17, so, with the help of his father, he constructed his own 24-fret model and dubbed it the Red Special. Its neck is made of solid mahogany, which was culled from the base of a 200-year old fireplace, and its body is solid oak. Three Burns single-coil pickups and a vibrato bar (whose springs were recycled from leftover motorcycle parts) rounded out this truly custom axe. In 1985, Guild began to market an authorized reproduction of the Red Special as their BM-1 model; May currently uses them as his backups. (The one and only original model remains, of course, his faithful Number One.)

For amplification, May relied on a classic tube-only Vox AC-30 and a mini 30-watt transistor amp fabricated by Queen member John Deacon that was also overloaded with a treble booster. And instead of traditional picks, May is well-known for strumming with a British six-pence piece, which resembles a U.S. nickel.

In late 1968, May hooked up with drummer Roger Taylor, and they formed an outfit known as Smile, who played London's pub and college circuit and even supported Pink Floyd on occasion. Smile recorded a one-off single in 1969 that promptly went nowhere, and they dissolved in early 1970. Taylor's friend, Freddie Bulsara (who would change his name to Freddie Mercury in honor of the mythological fleet-footed messenger of the gods), soon joined the fold. His enthusiasm for extravaganza, showmanship and musicianship were highly contagious. Queen were officially knighted in April 1970; May wanted to call the group Grand Dance, and Taylor wanted The Rich Kids, but, of course, the persuasive Mercury got his way, and so Queen it was. The three took their time hashing out ideas for the group's direction over the course of 1970, and finally, in February 1971, they added bassist John Deacon to the lineup. Queen was now primed to take on the world.

Their big break come in September 1971, when De Lane Lea Recording Studios in Wembley (which is located in North London) opened its doors. To attract clients, the studio wanted a hard-rock band to be on the premises to give hands-on demonstrations. In return for their services, Queen was granted unlimited and unbilled studio time *and* was allowed to keep the tapes of anything and everything they recorded. They tracked demo after demo, immersing themselves in the cutting edge of recording technology of the day; their insider knowledge quite obviously manifested itself in many of the band's well-arranged and well-produced tracks over the years. Roy Thomas Baker and John Anthony, engineers at nearby Trident Studios, became enamored with the group, and soon inked a contract with them. Queen now had a 24-track studio at its disposal-albeit during "dead" time, whenever it wasn't in use.

In 1973, their self-titled debut, *Queen,* hit the shops, led by an infectious single, "Keep Yourself Alive." Many mistook May's massive orchestral attack on *Queen* to be the work of synthesizers, which was certainly not the case (though the band would experiment with them during much of the '80s). *Queen II* followed in early 1974, and it became highly influential, especially thanks to the harmonic masterpiece "Seven Seas of Rhye." Nuno Bettencourt has gone on record as saying that *Queen II* is "my favorite album. It was so far ahead of its time."

Photo by Johnny Olson/RETNA LTD.

Next up was early 1975s *Sheer Heart Attack*, most notable for containing "Killer Queen," the bands breakthrough mainstream success. May's three-part solo – "each part has its own voice," as he's noted in interviews – was a clear precursor to the explosive tone evident later in "We Will Rock You;" the song is also littered with killer harmonies and stunning single-note phrases. At the time of recording *Heart Attack*, May had been recovering from a nasty bout with hepatitis when suddenly he had to be rushed to the hospital to have emergency surgery for a duodenal ulcer. May was convinced that the band was going to replace him while he was laid up (they weren't); instead, they left space for him on the tracks, and, when he was able to return to the studio, he attacked his parts with a vengeance.

There is no question that May and the boys reached their peak with late 1975's *A Night At the Opera* (named in honor of the Marx Brothers), and its commanding "Bohemian Rhapsody." The band had been experimenting like mad with multitracking, orchestration, arrangements, and guitar-vocal interplay. A compositional masterstroke, the 6-minute "Rhapsody" was a realization of the tenor Mercury's operatic dream, as well as a grand testament to May's own formidable arranging skills.

It took 3 full weeks of recording (7 days on the vocals alone), 180 vocal overdubs, and what seemed like just as many guitar overdubs to complete "Rhapsody." The song essentially breaks down into four major sections: the intro and main song sequence, a vocal-dominated operatic interlude, May's showcase section, and a reprise of the intro and main sequence. May enters the song around 2:19 with a doubled melodic line, and when his epic diatonic solo commences 15 seconds later, a third guitar is added to the mix. May pulls out all the stops, cagily placing a double-timed phrase in the middle of the solo to serve as the midpoint's climax. The song's third section moves along in a 12/8 shuffle groove that's syncopated in E♭ major. When the fourth section arrives, May's harmonic interplay takes center stage, as he joins his four guitars with three additional counterlines; this motif can be heard all over the canons of the likes of Yngwie Malmsteen and George Lynch.

And, as the legendary story goes, the song was almost completely *lost!* "Rhapsody" was done entirely on 16-track, and the tape quickly started to wear thin. After noticing a significant loss in the song's top end, the tape was inspected and discovered to be almost totally transparent, as all of its oxide had rubbed off. As May himself noted, "It was time to hurriedly make a copy and get on with it." Got on with it they did—and "Rhapsody" was an immediate smash, sitting atop of the charts for 9 straight weeks. (Many years later, "Rhapsody" gained an un-expected resurgence in popularity thanks to its prominence in the popular Mike Myers-Dana Carvey comedy film, 1991s *Wayne's World*.)

Photo by Fin Costello/RETNA LTD.

4

A *Day at the Races* followed in 1976, and though it didn't quite carry the weight of *Opera*, it certainly had it moments, including "Tie Your Mother Down," with its emphasis on double-tracked guitar, vibrato-bar feedback, and a keen slide solo, and "Somebody to Love," with its juicy, thickly layered tone.

But the next milestone came with 1977s *News of the World* and the incredible one-two punch of "We Will Rock You" and "We Are the Champions," which have become long-renowned sporting-event staples. *World* was the first album where May began to downplay his layering techniques, signifying the band's changing directions. But that didn't mean May was throwing in the towel, as the violent, fuzzed-out chords in the outgoing "Rock You" solo readily proves. And then there's "Champions," another May showcase that's chock-full of chordal arpeggios and pentatonic single-note lines that are accented with a flange effect. May has taken care to point out that besides the fact that there are no drums on "We Will Rock You," people always seem to mix up the stamp-and-clap routine: "People tend to do three claps rather than the two stamps and a clap that it is." (Consider yourself notified.)

1978s *Jazz* contained the controversial "Fat Bottomed Girls" (the phrase "politically correct" hadn't been invented yet, but it would certainly have applied to the furor that followed the song's release) and "Bicycle Race," a proggy throwback of sorts with trills and pans galore. Around this time, though, some band members expressed a desire to pursue more rhythmical ideas in Queen's music. 1980s *The Game* saw to that concept in spades. *The Game* kicked off with the rockabilly-tinged "Crazy Little Thing Called Love," with May doing his best James Burton impersonation by wrangling a vintage Fender Telecaster during the solo section. (Mercury himself strummed rhythm guitar on the track.) But it was John Deacon's thumping "Another One Bites the Dust," fueled by his hypnotic bass line, that broke the bank, topping the rock, disco and soul charts in the States. On "Dust" May wisely played to the strength of the song, limiting his input mostly to jangly background accompaniment.

Throughout the '80s Queen's stature as one of the globe's top acts continued to rise (though their profile in the States diminished somewhat), peaking in 1986, when half a million fans applied for tickets to the band's two shows at Wembley stadium. Wembley was also the site for April 1992s Freddie Mercury Tribute Concert, which showcased the talents of Metallica, Def Leppard, Robert Plant, Elton John, David Bowie and scores of others. A final Queen album, titled *Made in Heaven*, which features vocal tracks that Mercury recorded in 1991, was released in late 1995. Through Mercury is gone, the unique legacy of Queen will certainly continue. Long live the Queen.

Photo by Arthur D'Amario/RETNA, LTD.

We Will Rock You

Words and Music by Brian May

Outro-Guitar Solo

We will, we will rock you.   Al-right.

We Are the Champions

Words and Music by Freddie Mercury

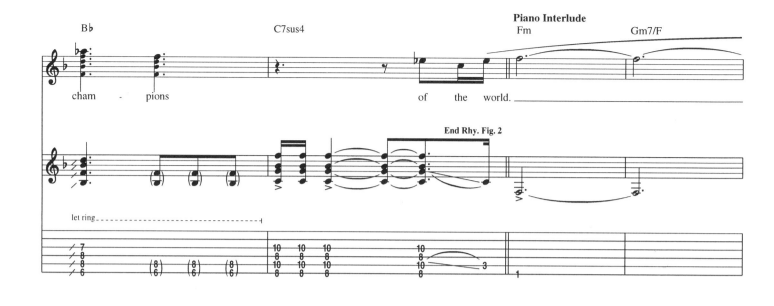

Another One Bites the Dust

Words and Music by John Deacon

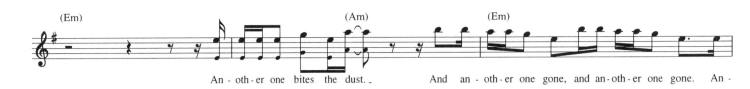

An-oth-er one bites the dust._ And an-oth-er one gone, and an-oth-er one gone. An-

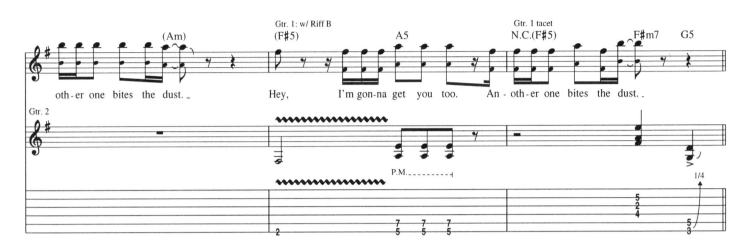

oth-er one bites the dust._ Hey, I'm gon-na get you too. An-oth-er one bites the dust._

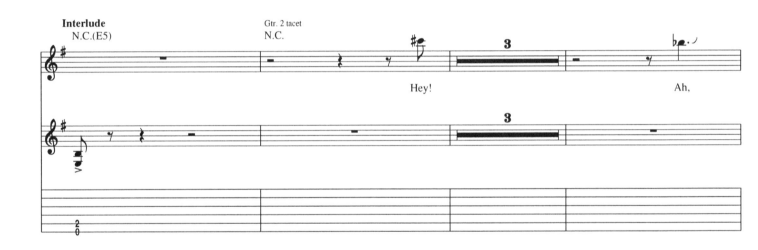

Hey! Ah,

take it! Bite the dust! _ Bite the dust, - ah!

Hey! An-oth-er one bites the dust._ An-

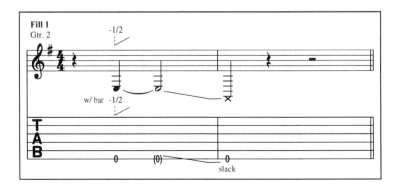

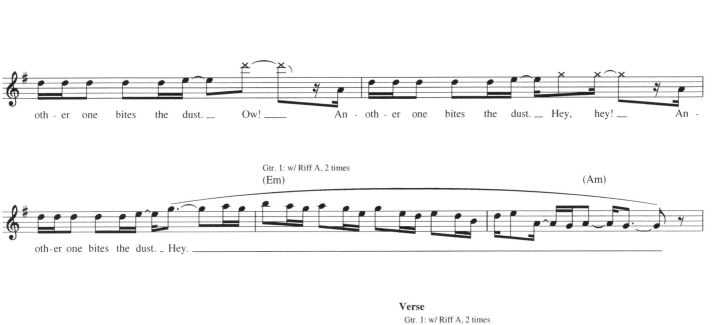

oth-er one bites the dust. __ Ow! ___ An - oth-er one bites the dust. __ Hey, hey! ___ An -

oth-er one bites the dust. __ Hey. _____

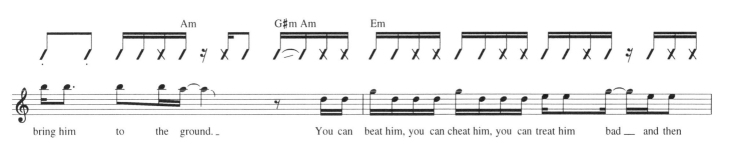

Ooh, __ shot! 3. There are plen-ty of ways _ that you can hurt a man _ and

bring him to the ground. _ You can beat him, you can cheat him, you can treat him bad __ and then

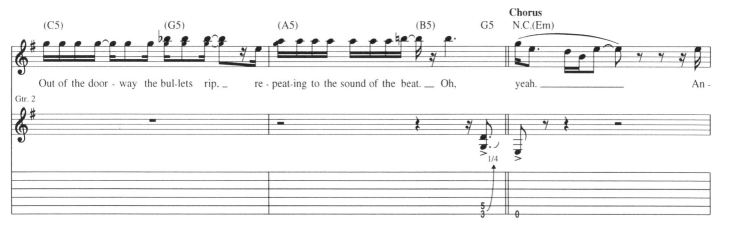

leave him when he's down, _ yeah. _ But I'm read-y. Yes, I'm read-y for you. _ I'm stand-in' on my own two feet. _

Out of the door - way the bul-lets rip, _ re - peat-ing to the sound of the beat. __ Oh, yeah. _____ An -

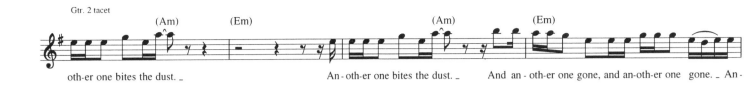

oth-er one bites the dust. ___ An-oth-er one bites the dust. ___ And an-oth-er one gone, and an-oth-er one gone. ___ An-

oth-er one bites the dust. ___ Hey, I'm gon-na get you too. An-oth-er one bites the dust. ___
(Yeah. _____)

Outro

Shoot-out! ___ Ay. _____

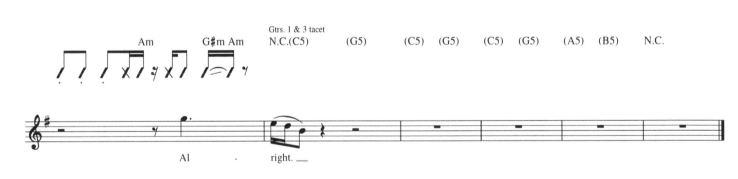

Al - right. ___

Killer Queen

Words and Music by Freddie Mercury

Verse

2. To a-void com-pli-ca-tions, she nev-er kept the same ad-dress.

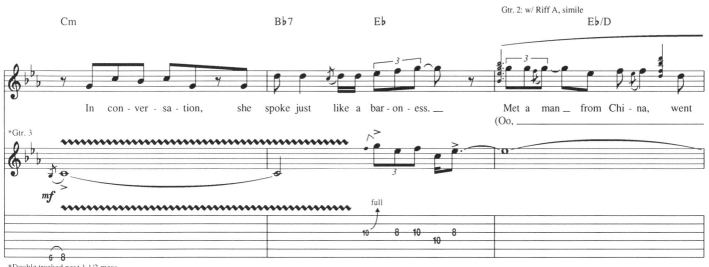

In con-ver-sa-tion, she spoke just like a bar-on-ess. __ Met a man __ from Chi-na, went
(Oo, __

*Gtr. 3

mf

*Double tracked next 1 1/2 meas.

down to Gei-sha Mi - nah, then a-gain in-ci-den-t'ly if you're
_____ a kill - er, kill - er, she's a

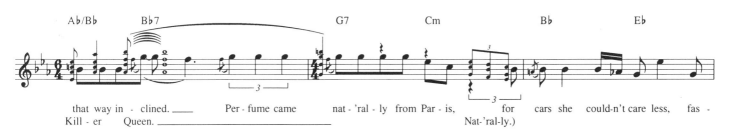

that way in - clined. ___ Per-fume came nat-'ral-ly from Par-is, for cars she could-n't care less, fas-
Kill - er Queen. ___ Nat-'ral-ly.)

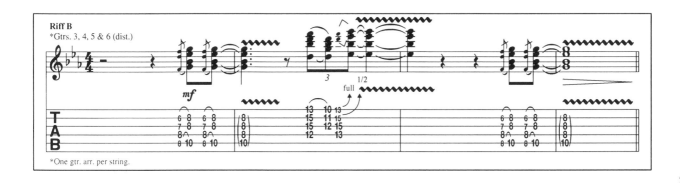

Riff B
*Gtrs. 3, 4, 5 & 6 (dist.)

mf

*One gtr. arr. per string.

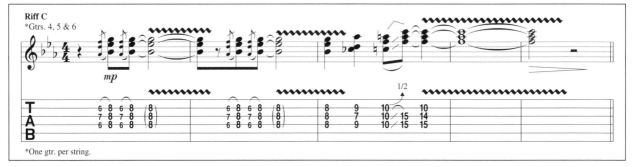

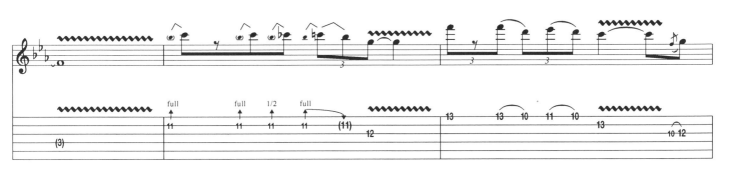

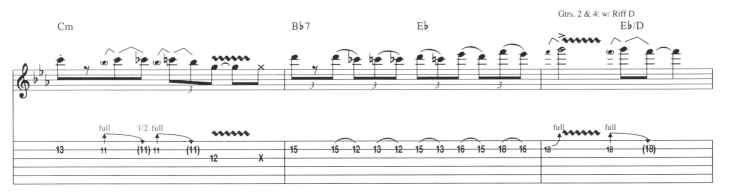

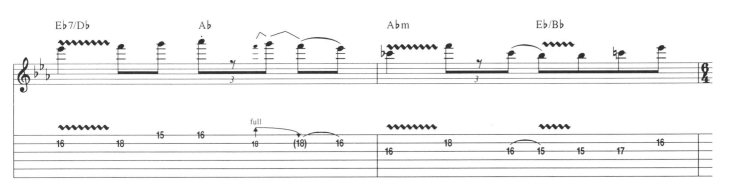

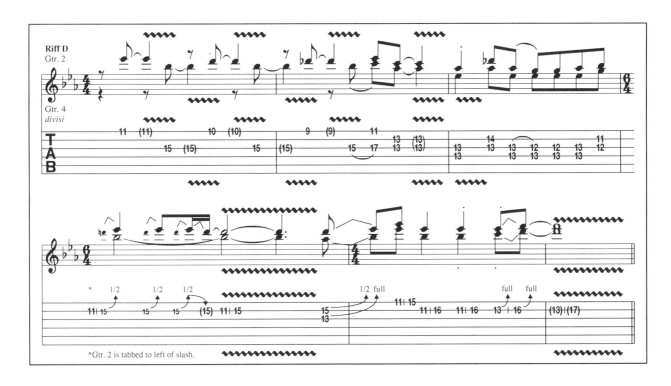

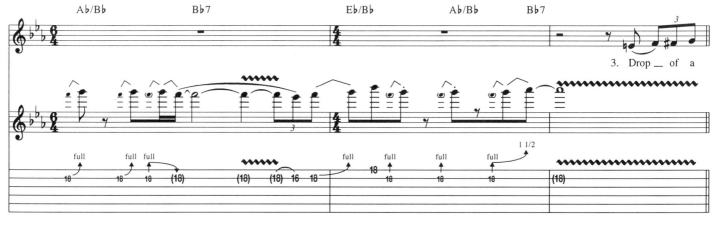

26

Somebody to Love

Words and Music by Freddie Mercury

28

Guitar Solo

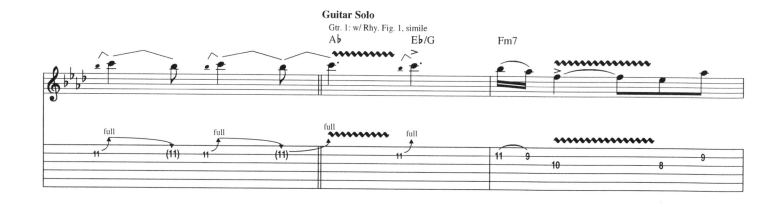

Gtrs. 5, 6 & 7 tacet

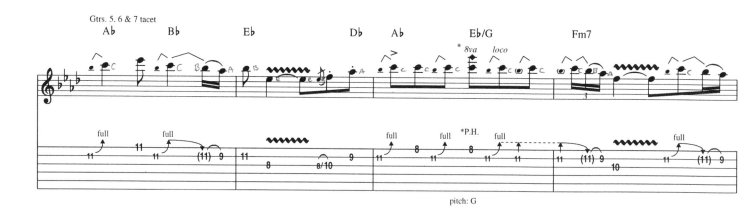

pitch: G

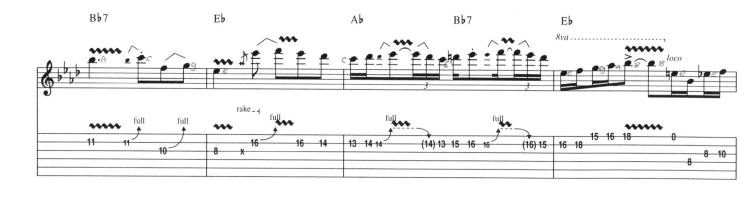

Chorus

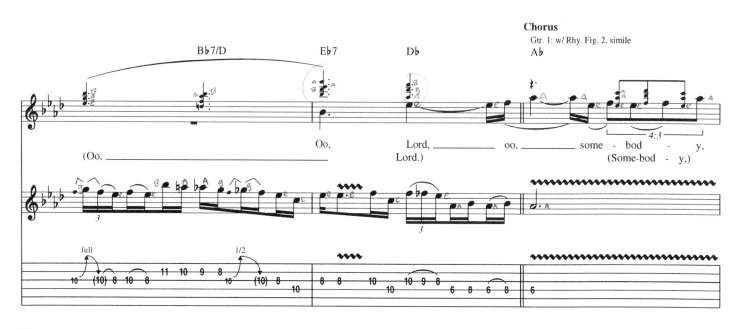

Gtr. 4 tacet

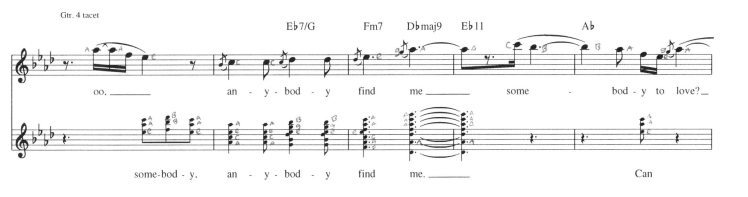

oo, _____ an - y - bod - y find me _____ some - bod - y to love?__

some-bod - y, an - y-bod - y find me. _____ Can

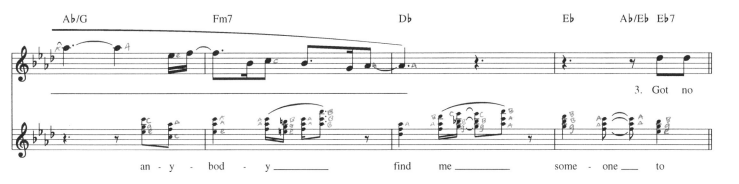

an - y - bod - y _____ find me _____ some - one ___ to

3. Got no

Verse

Gtr. 1: w/ Rhy. Fig. 1. simile

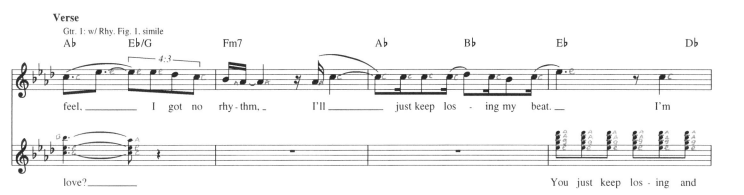

feel, _____ I got no rhy - thm, __ I'll _____ just keep los - ing my beat. __ I'm

love?_____ You just keep los - ing and

Gtr. 4: w/ Fill 2

O. K., I'm al - right. I ain't gon-na face _____ no de - feat. __ I just

los - ing. He's al - right, he's al - right, _____ yeah, __ yeah.

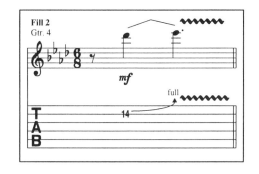

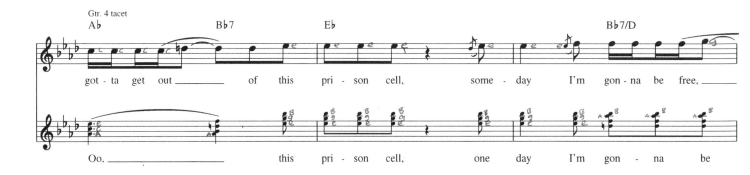

got-ta get out _____ of this pri-son cell, some-day I'm gon-na be free,

Oo, _____ this pri-son cell, one day I'm gon-na be

Chorus

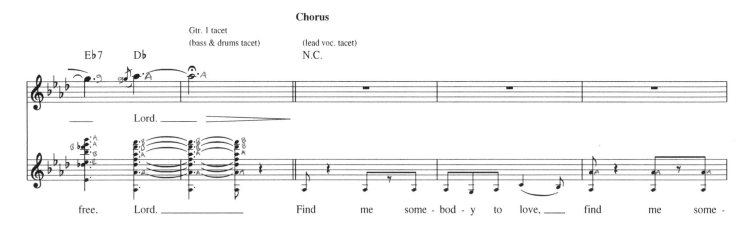

free, Lord. _____ Find me some-bod-y to love, _____ find me some-

bod-y to love, _____ find me some-bod-y to love, _____ find me some-

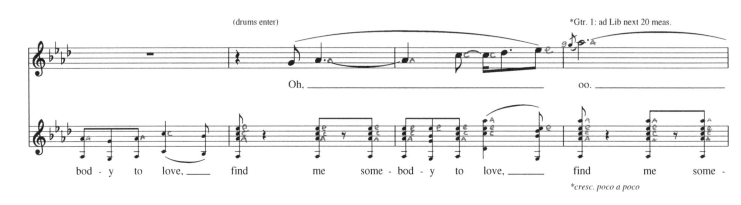

Oh, _____ oo. _____

Find _____ me, find _____ me, find. _____

bod-y to love, _____ find me (me) some-bod-y to love, _____ find me (me) some-

Oo, _____ find

bod-y to love, _____ find me (me) some-bod-y to love, _____ find me (me) some-bod-y to love, _____

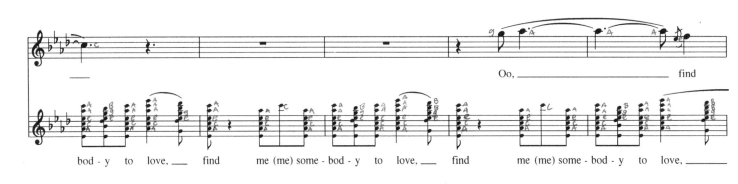

me, find me some-bod-y to love. ___ Oo. ___

___ find me (me) some-bod-y to love, ___ find me (me) some-bod-y to love, ___

some-bod-y, some-bod-y, some-bod-y, some-bod-y, some-bod-y, find me some-bod-y, find me some-

Rubato

Gtr. 1 tacet
(bass & drums tacet)

| Ab | Eb/G | Fm7 | Dbmaj9 | Eb11 | N.C. |

Gtr. 1

Can an-y-bod-y find me ___ some-bod-y to ___

bod-y to love. An-y-bod-y find me. ___

Outro-Chorus
A Tempo
Gtr. 1: w/ Rhy. Fig. 3, 7 times, simile

| Ab | Ab/G | Fm7 |

love? ___

Bkgd. Voc. Fig. 4

Find me some-bod-y

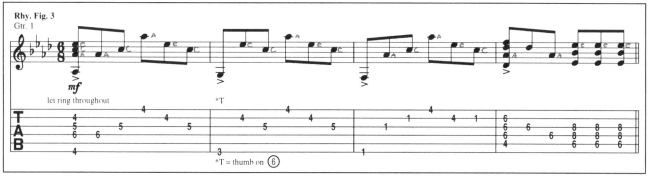

Rhy. Fig. 3
Gtr. 1

mf

let ring throughout   *T

*T = thumb on ⑥

35

Fat Bottomed Girls

Words and Music by Brian May

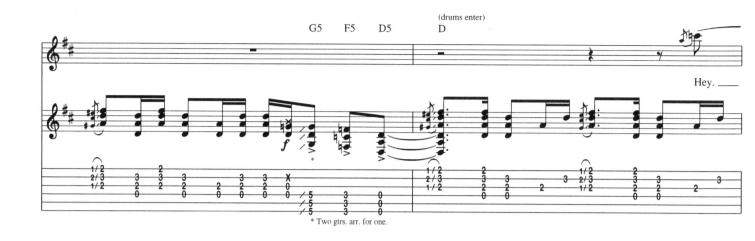

* Two gtrs. arr. for one.

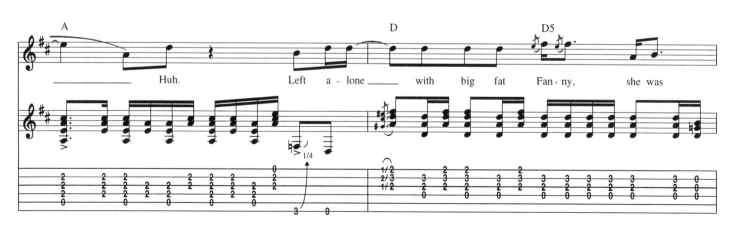

sing-in' with my band 'cross the wa - ter, 'cross the land, _ I seen ev - 'ry blue-eyed floo - zy on the way. _

_____ Hey. But their beau - ty and their style _ went kind of smooth _ af - ter a while, _ take me to _

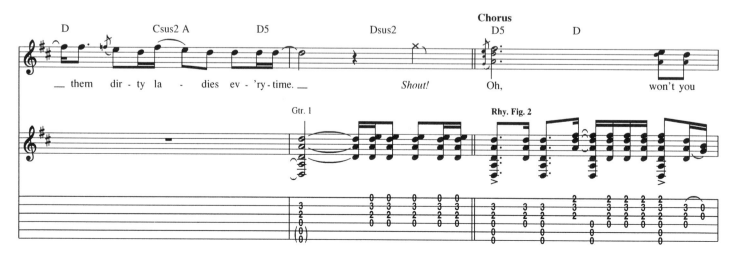

_ them dirt - ty la - dies ev - 'ry - time. _ Shout! Oh, won't you

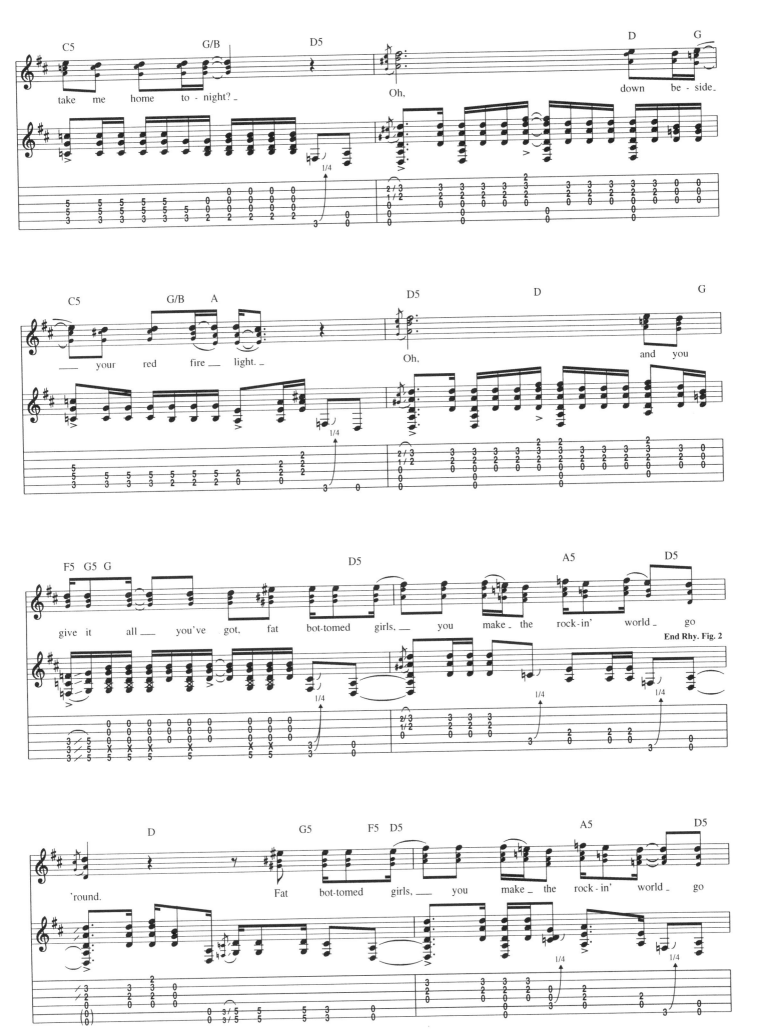

Gtr. 3: w/ Fill 1

Csus2

Oo, _____ yeah, _____ uh. Oh, yeah.

Them fat bot-tomed girls, they get me. Yeah, yeah,
(Fat bot-tomed girls. ___)

* 2nd gtr. simile (next 6 meas.)

D

yeah. Al - right, ride 'em cow-boy._

Fill 1
Gtr. 3

mp

full

full full full full

full

full full

1/4

Bicycle Race

Words and Music by Freddie Mercury

*Piano arr. for gtr.

**Chord symbols represent overall tonality.

***Harmonies dbld. *8ba* in most cases, throughout.

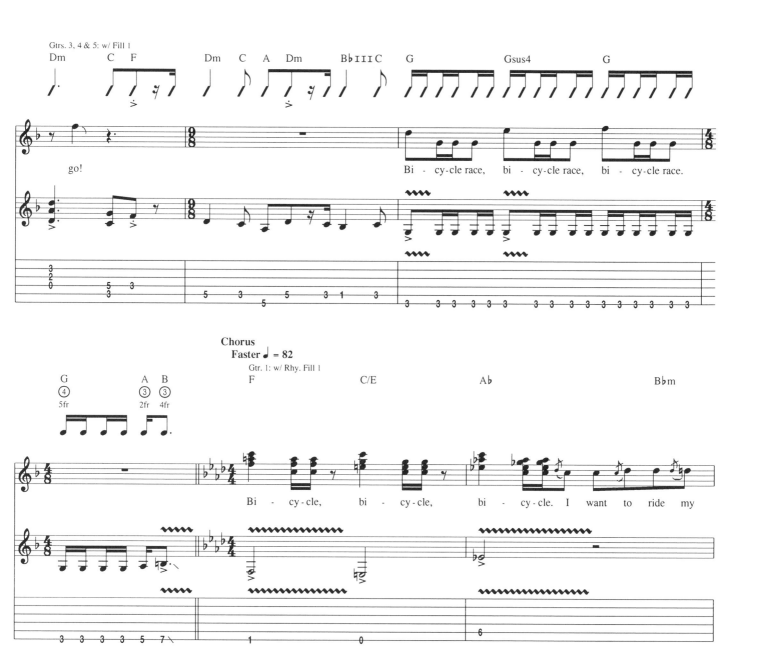

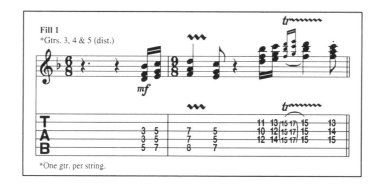

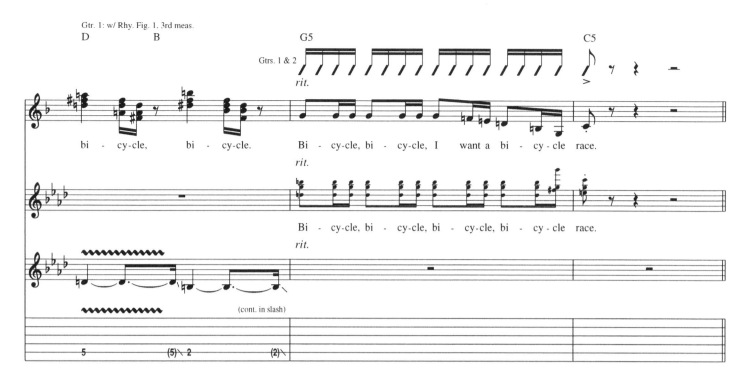

bi - cy-cle, bi - cy-cle. Bi - cy-cle, bi - cy-cle, I want a bi - cy - cle race.

Bi - cy-cle, bi - cy-cle, bi - cy-cle, bi - cy-cle race.

Interlude

Faster ♩ = 172

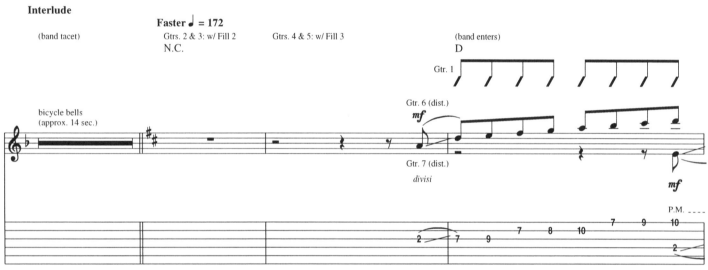

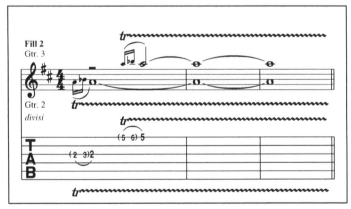

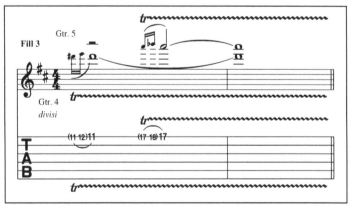

You're My Best Friend

Words and Music by John Deacon

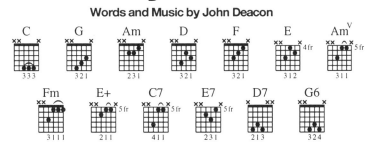

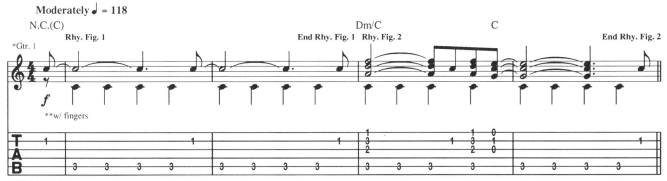

Intro
Moderately ♩ = 118

* Kybds. arr. for gtr.

** Keep pick in palm of hand.

Chorus

Ooh, you make me live. ___ What-ev-er this world can give to me, ___ it's you, ___ you're all I ___ see.

___ Ooh, you make me live, ___ now, hon-ey. Ooh, you make me live. ___

1. Oh, ___ you're the best ___ friend that I ___ ev-er had. ___ I've been with you such a

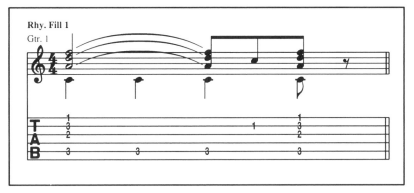

long time. __ You're my sun - shine, and I want __ you to know __ that my feel - ings are

true. _ I real - ly love _____ you. __ Oh, __ you're my best __ friend. _____
(Ooh. _)

Bridge

Ooh, _ I've been wan - der - in' _ round. ____ Still come back to you. _
Ooh, you make me live. ____ A - round. _ Ooh.

And in rain or shine __ you've stood by me, girl. ___ I'm
Still come back to you, _____ girl. __ I'm

hap - py at home. ____ You're my best __ friend. _____
hap - py. _____ Hap - py at home. ___

54

Chorus
Gtr. 1: w/ Rhy. Fig. 2, 4 times

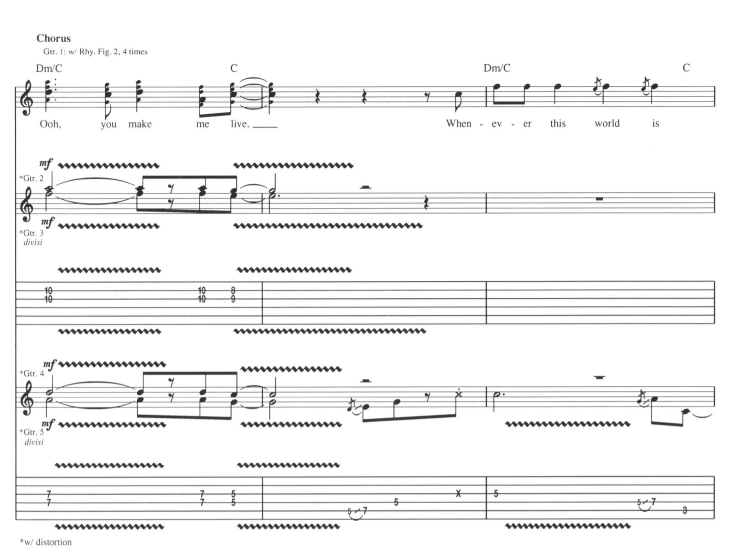

Ooh, you make me live. _____   When - ev - er this world is

*w/ distortion

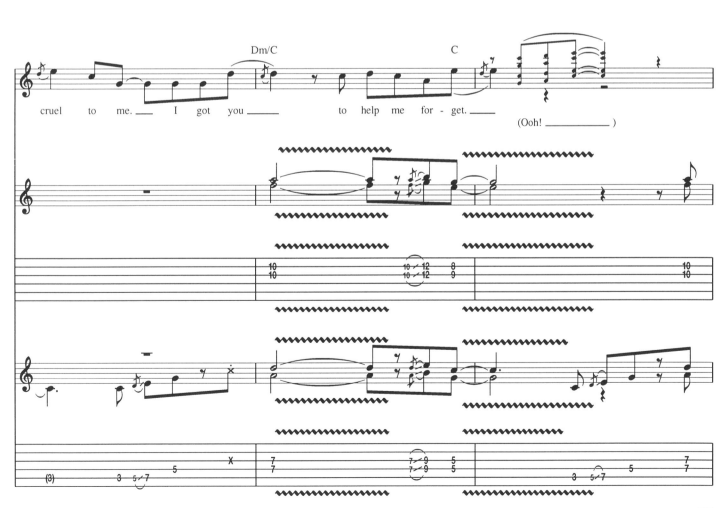

cruel to me. _____ I got you _____   to help me for - get. _____
(Ooh! _____)

Interlude

*1st chord is tied, not struck.

** For the next 4 meas.,
Gtr. 2 is indicated to
right of slashes in TAB.

Outro

Crazy Little Thing Called Love

Words and Music by Freddie Mercury

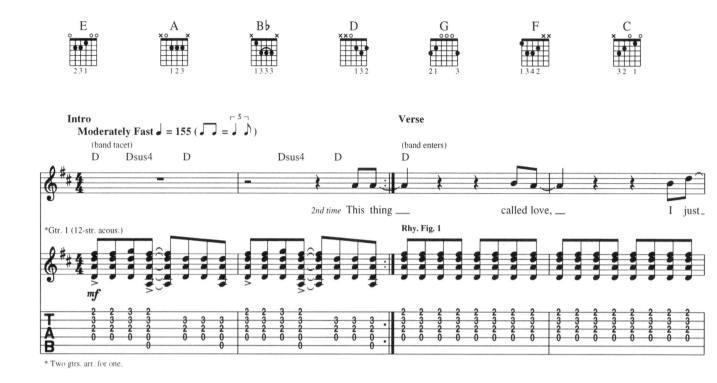

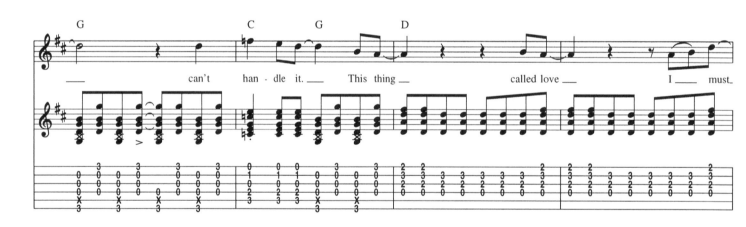

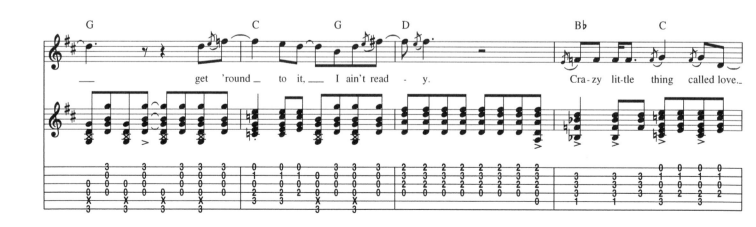

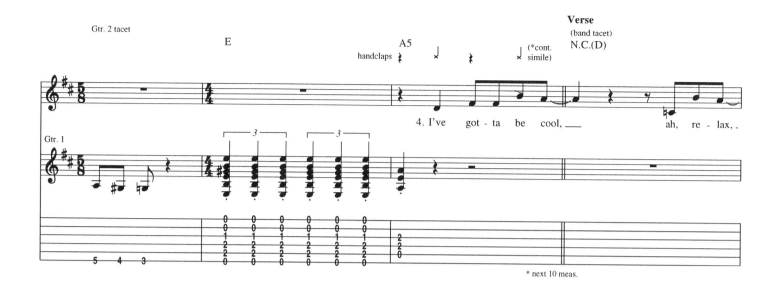

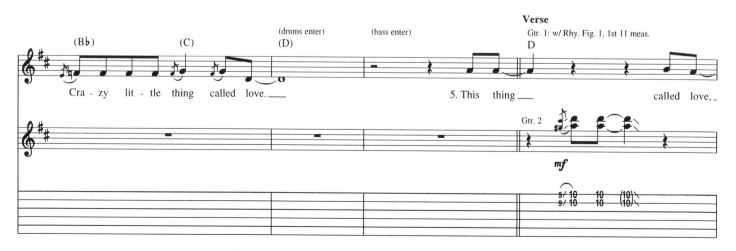

(Yeah, yeah.)

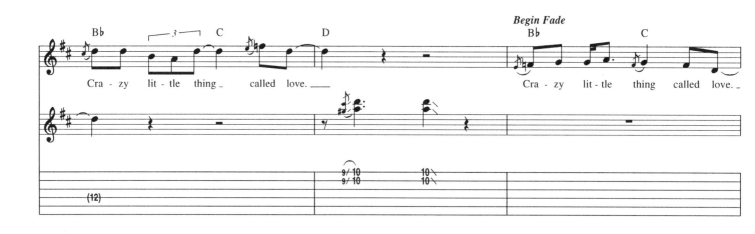

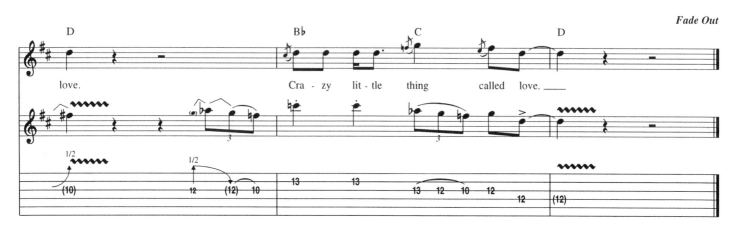

Now I'm Here

Words and Music by Brian May

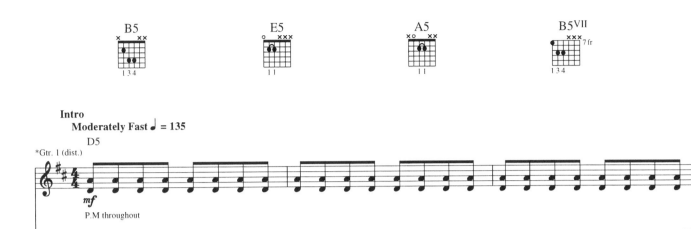

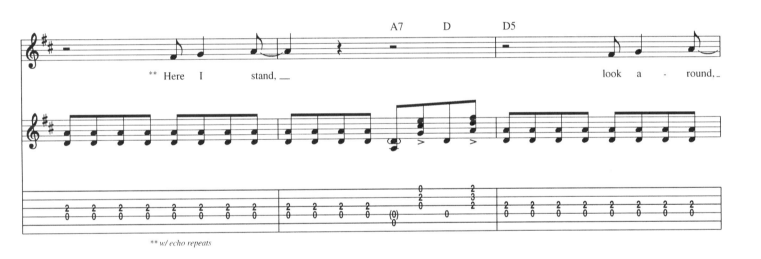

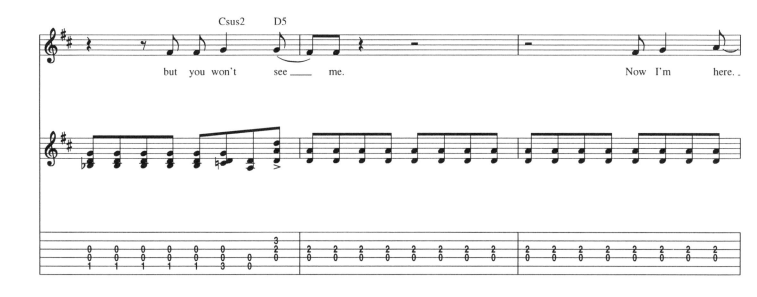

but you won't see ___ me.   Now I'm   here.

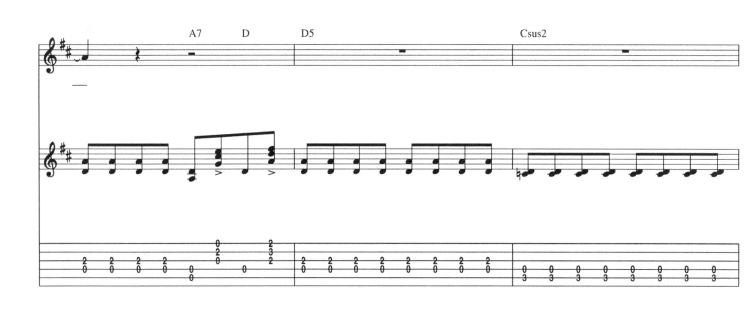

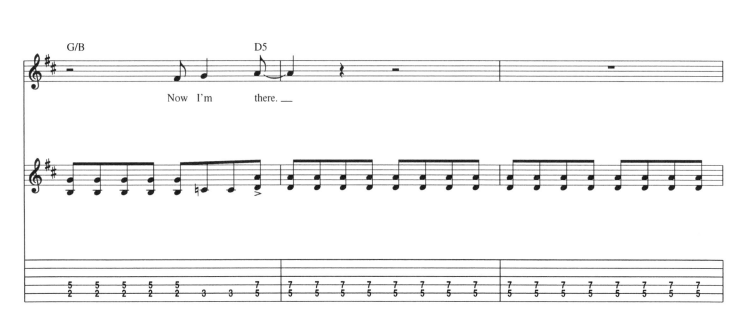

Now I'm   there. ___

Gtr. 2: w/ Fill 1

Csus2   G/B   A   Asus4

I'm just a,

*discontinue P.M.

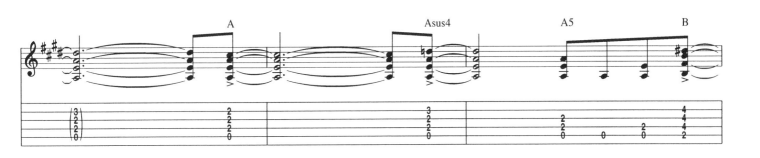

A   Asus4   A5   B

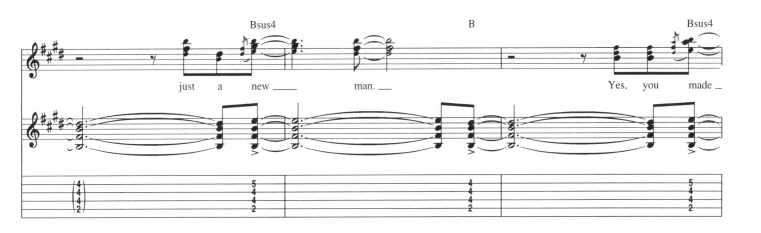

Bsus4   B   Bsus4

just a new ____ man. ____   Yes, you made ___

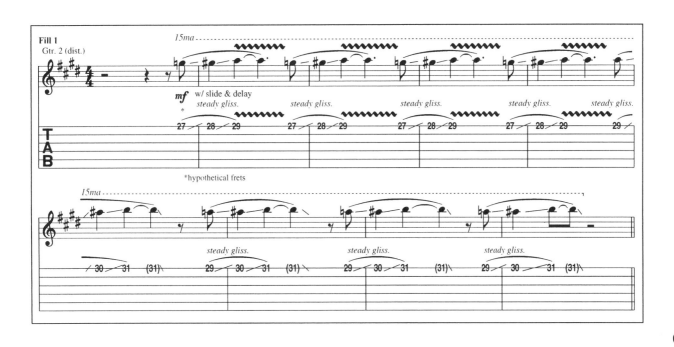

Fill 1
Gtr. 2 (dist.)

15ma

mf w/ slide & delay
steady gliss.   *steady gliss.*   *steady gliss.*   *steady gliss.*   *steady gliss.*

*hypothetical frets

15ma

steady gliss.   *steady gliss.*   *steady gliss.*

69

me live a - gain. ____ Wow!

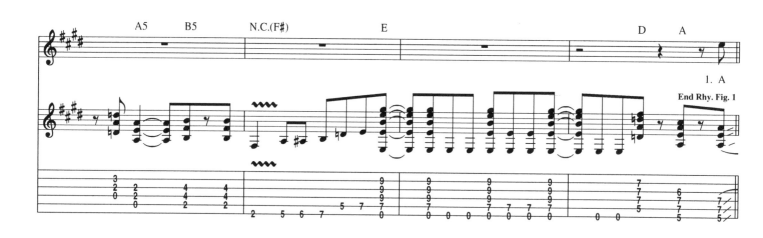

I. A

ba - by I was when you took my hand, _ and the light of the night _ burned bright. _

*Chord symbols reflect basic tonality.

The peo - ple all stared, did - n't un - der - stand, _ but you

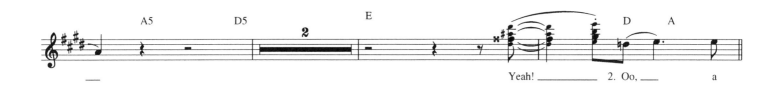

Verse

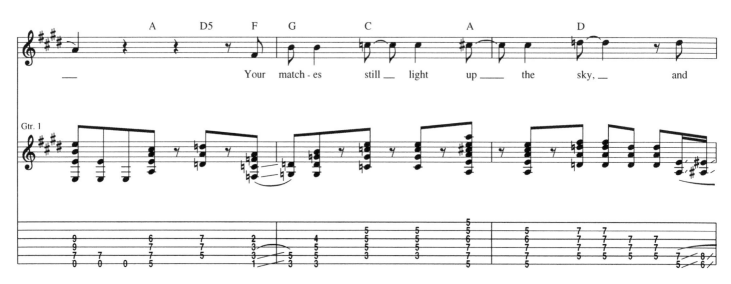

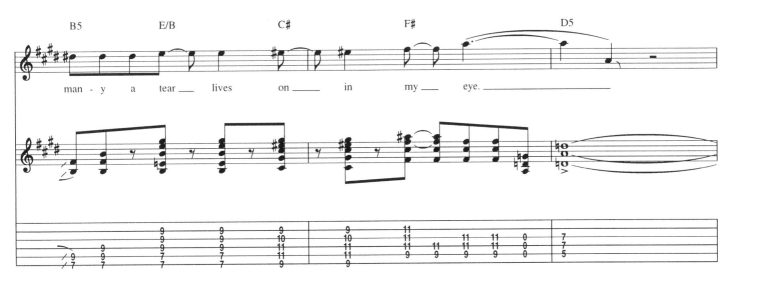

man- - y a tear ___ lives on ___ in my ___ eye. _____

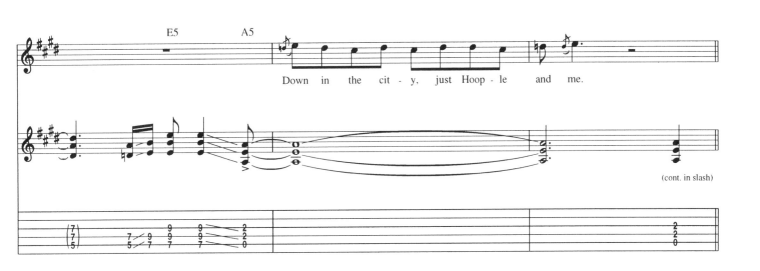

Down in the cit - y, just Hoop - le and me.

(cont. in slash)

Chorus

Gtr. 1: w/ Rhy. Fig. 3, 7 times, simile

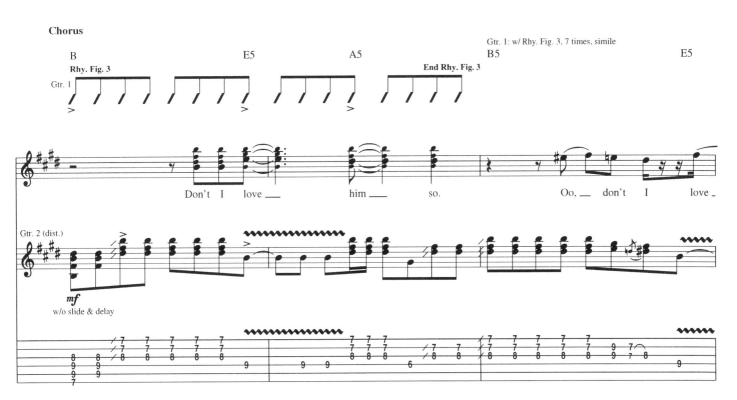

Rhy. Fig. 3

End Rhy. Fig. 3

Gtr. 1

Don't I love ___ him ___ so. Oo, ___ don't I love __

Gtr. 2 (dist.)

mf

w/o slide & delay

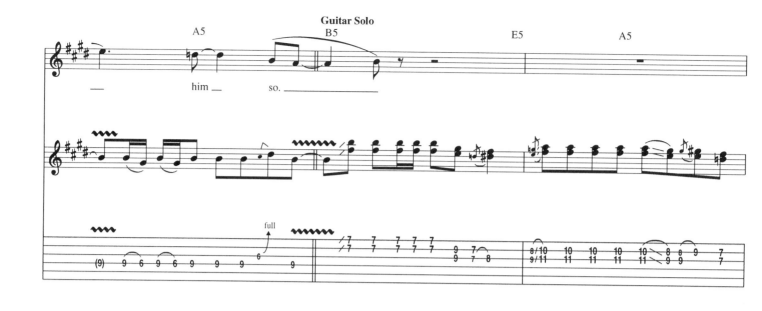

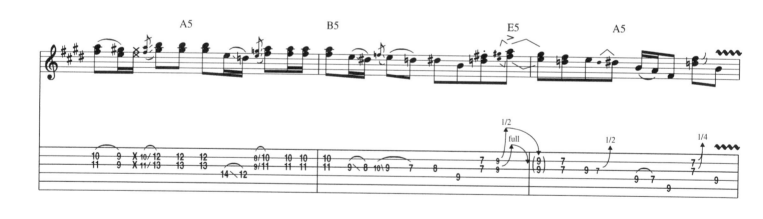

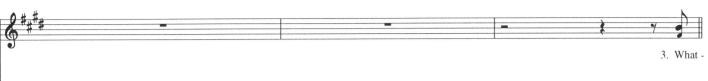
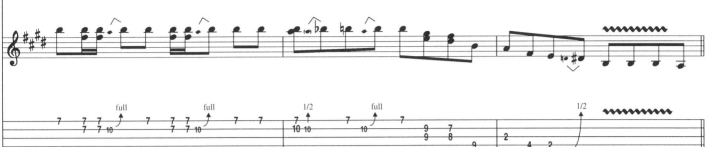

Verse

Bridge

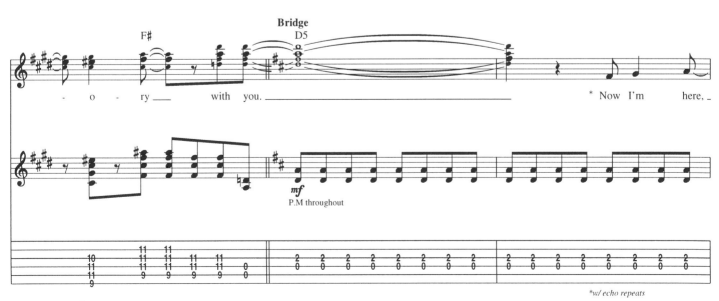

w/ echo repeats

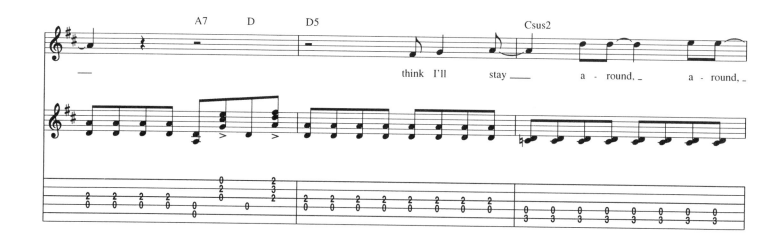

think I'll stay ___ a - round, _ a - round, _

a - round, _ a - round, _____ a - round, _ a - round. _

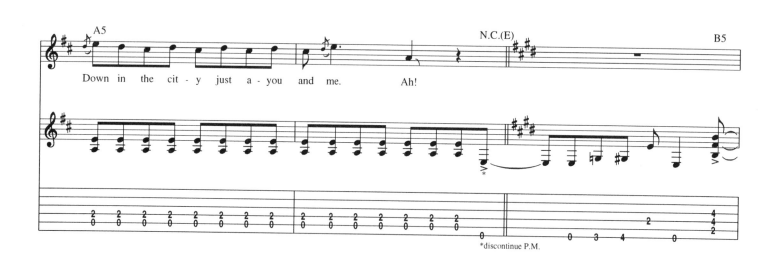

Down in the cit - y just a - you and me. Ah!

*discontinue P.M.

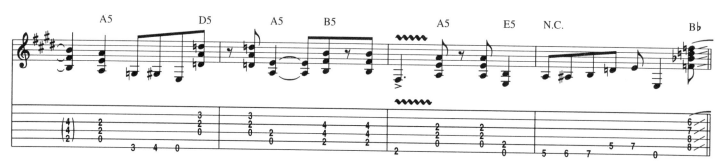

Outro

B   E   B   N.C.(E)   A   Bb   B5^{VIII}

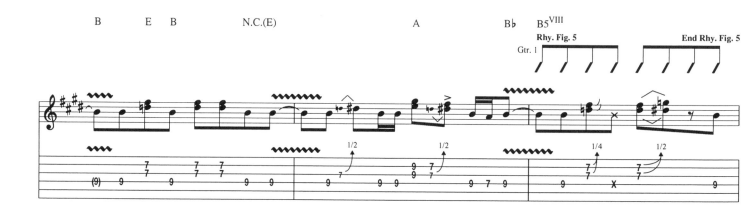

Gtr. 1: w/ Rhy. Fig. 5, simile, till end
w/ Bkgd. Voc. Fig. 1

Begin Fade

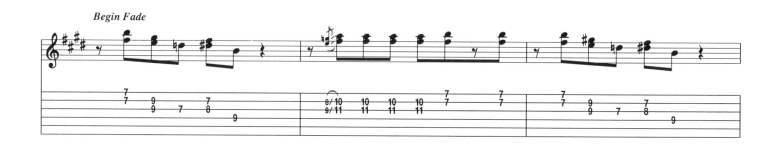

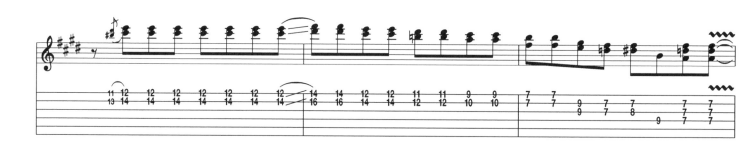

Fade Out

Bkgd. Voc. Fig. 1

(Go,   go, ____   go, _____   lit - tle queen - ie.)

Play the Game

Words and Music by Freddie Mercury

Gtr. 1 tacet

Fmaj7   F   Dm   G   C/G   Em

gun.   Love runs from my   head down   to my   toes.   My   love   is   pump-in' through my   veins,   (Play   the game

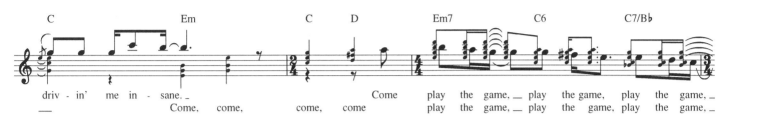

C   Em   C   D   Em7   C6   C7/B♭

driv-in'   me in-sane.   Come   play   the game, play   the game, play   the game,

Come,   come,   come, come   play   the game, play   the game, play   the game,

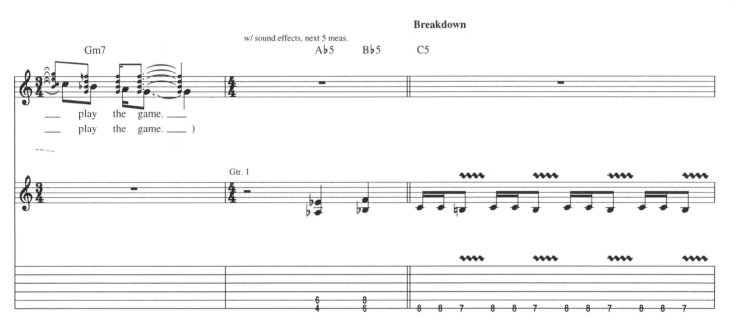

Breakdown

w/ sound effects, next 5 meas.

Gm7   A♭5   B♭5   C5

play   the   game.

play   the   game.   )

Gtr. 1

B♭5   A5   **Guitar Solo**   A♭5   C5

Gtr. 1

Gtr. 2

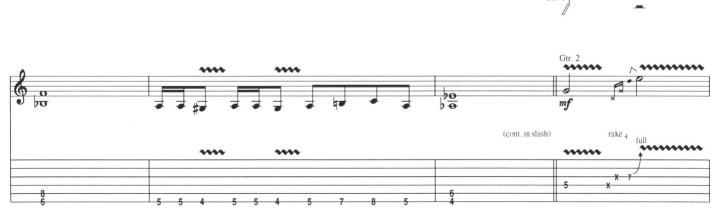

mf

(cont. in slash)   rake   full

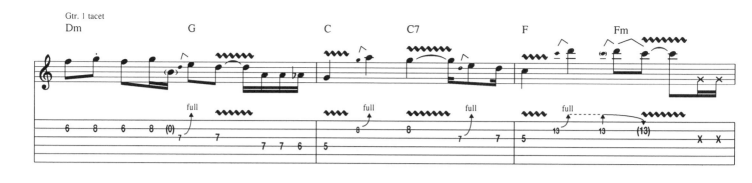

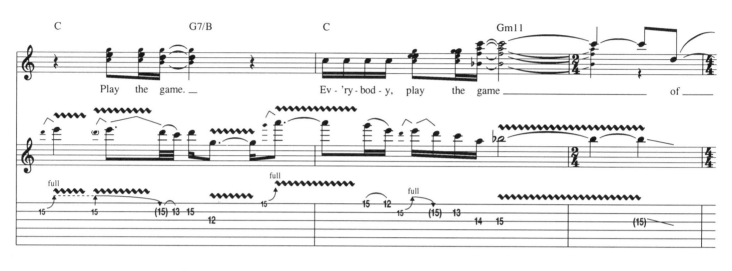

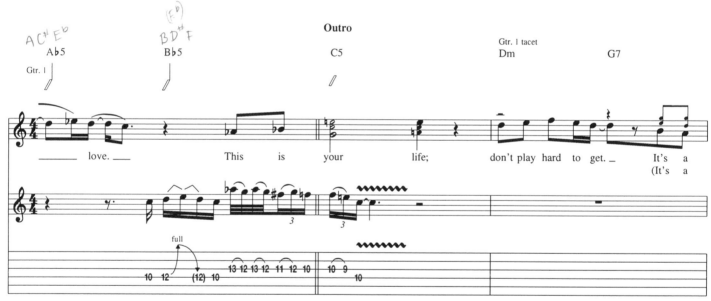

Seven Seas of Rhye

Words and Music by Freddie Mercury

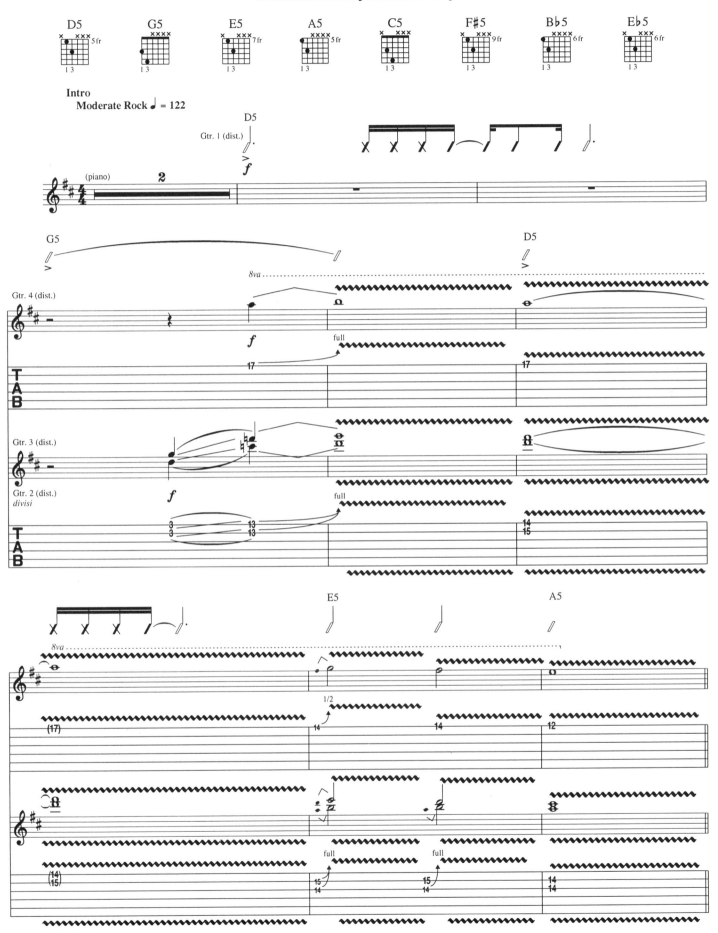

Verse

Gtrs. 2, 3 & 4 tacet

Verse

Gtr. 1: w/ Rhy. Fig. 1

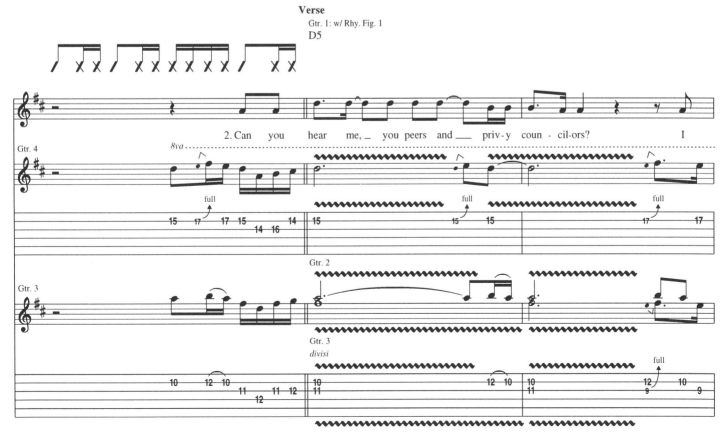

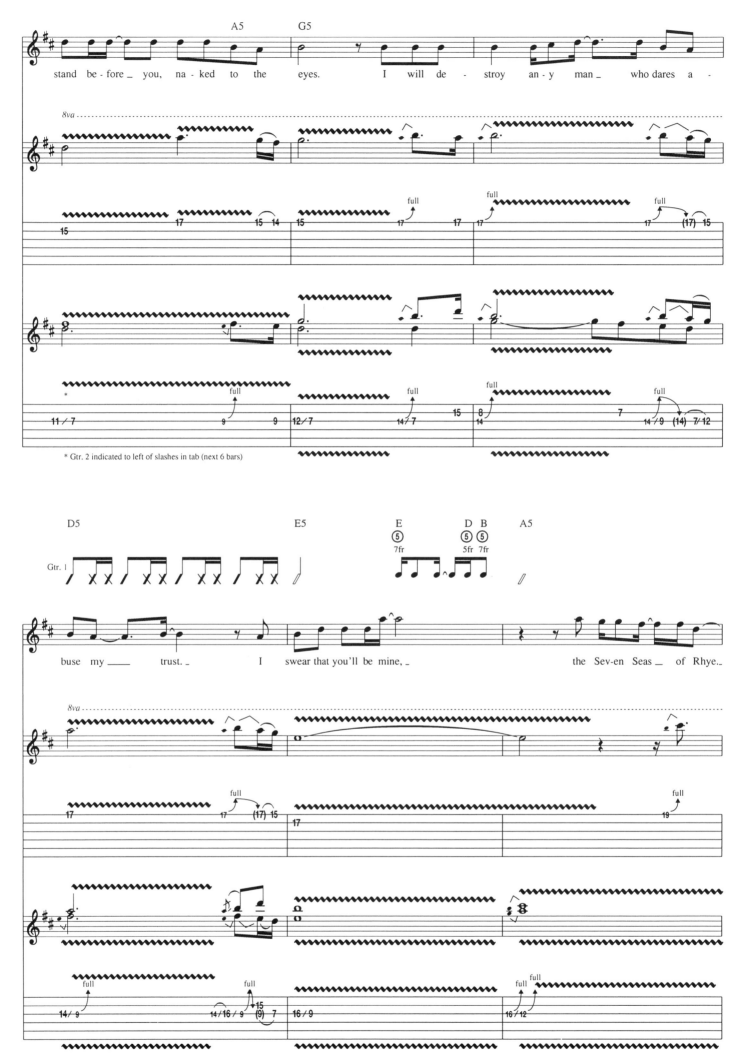

* Gtr. 2 indicated to left of slashes in tab (next 6 bars)

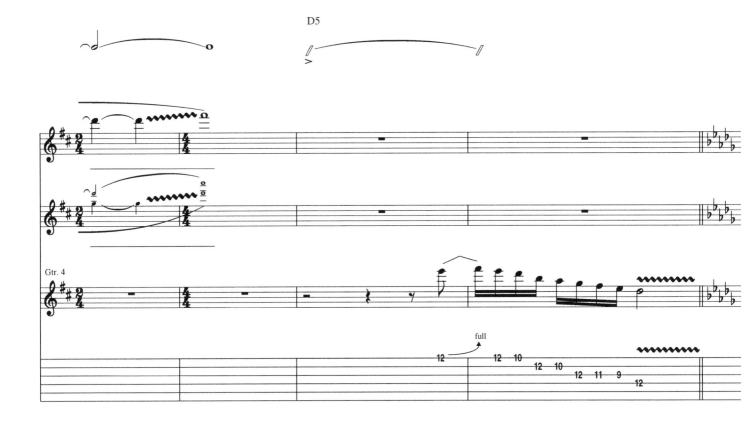

Guitar Solo

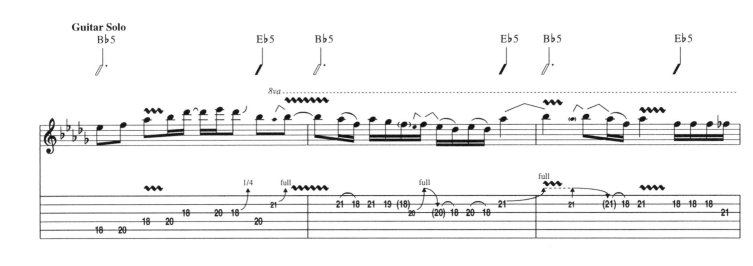

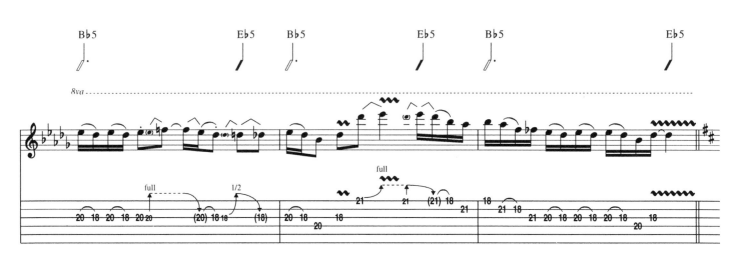

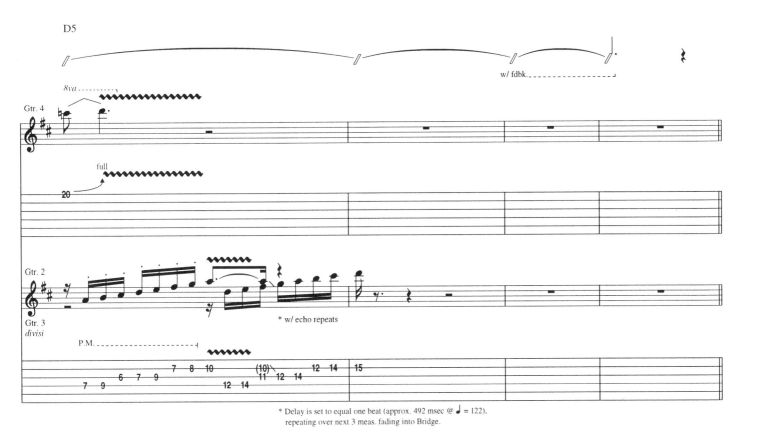

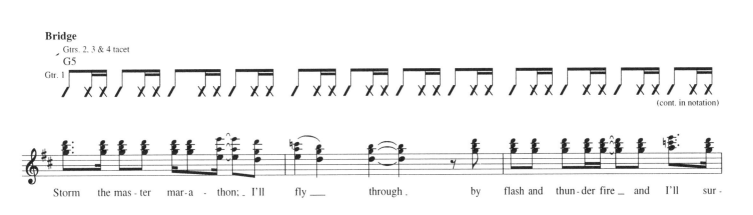

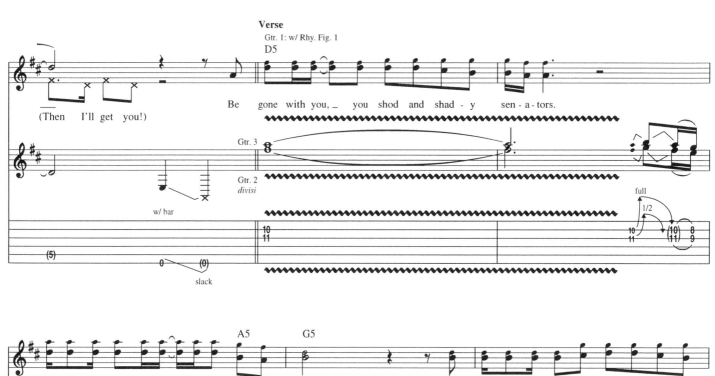

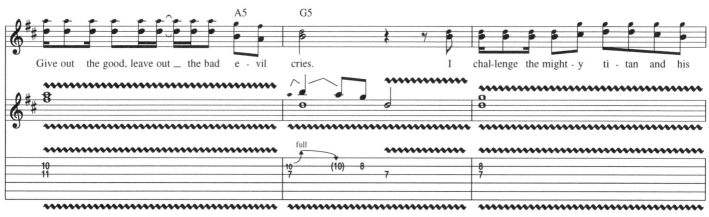

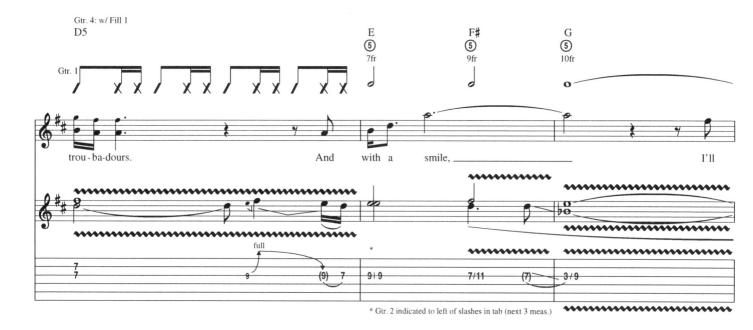

* Gtr. 2 indicated to left of slashes in tab (next 3 meas.)

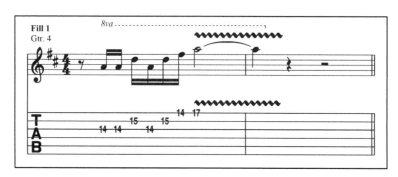

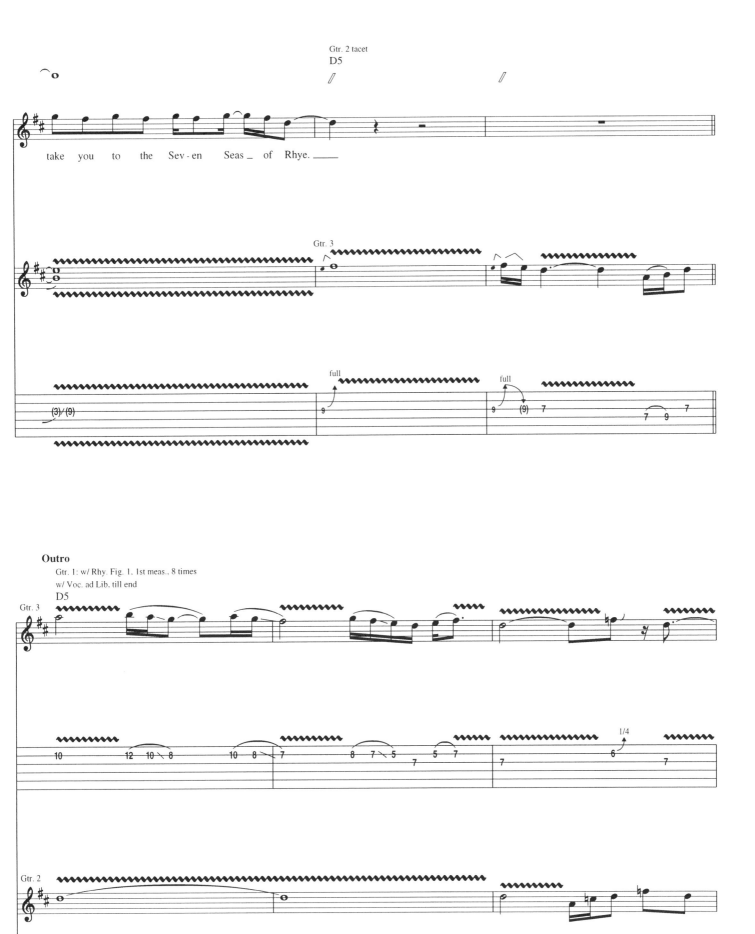

take you to the Sev - en Seas __ of Rhye. _____

Outro

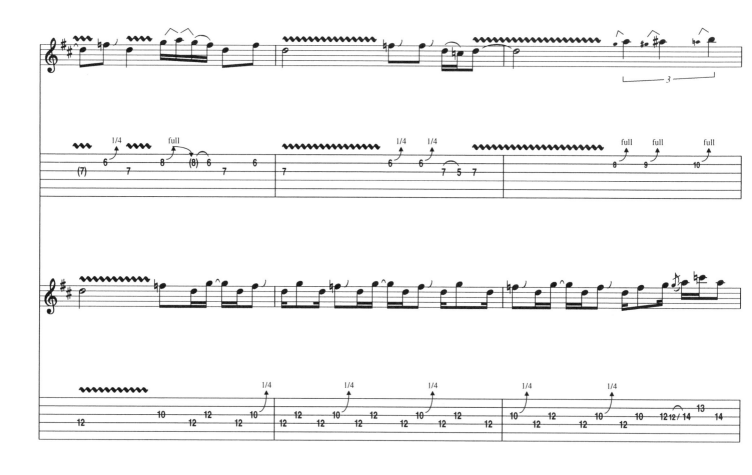

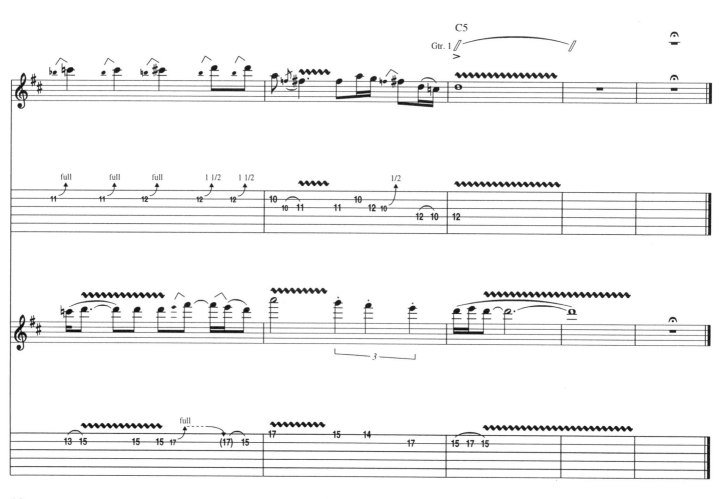

Body Language

Words and Music by Freddie Mercury

Gtr. 1; Drop D Tuning:
① = E ④ = D
② = B ⑤ = A
③ = G ⑥ = D

* Keyboard arr. for gtr.

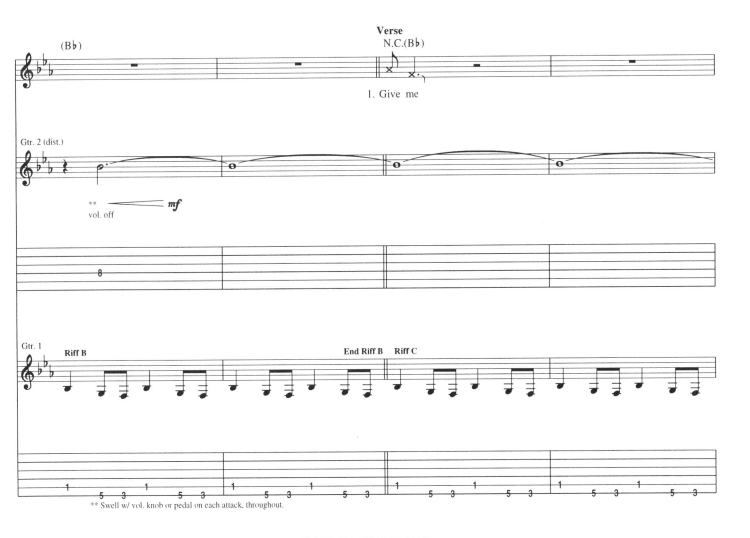

** Swell w/ vol. knob or pedal on each attack, throughout.

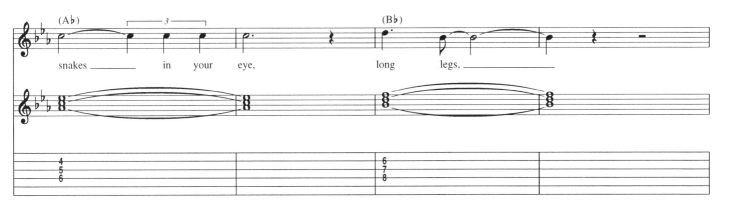

snakes _____ in your eye, long legs, _____

Gtr. 2 tacet
(Ab)   (Db)

great thighs. _ You've got the cut-est ass ____ I've ev-er seen. ___ Knock me

(Cb)   (Eb5)

down for a six ____ an-y-time. ____

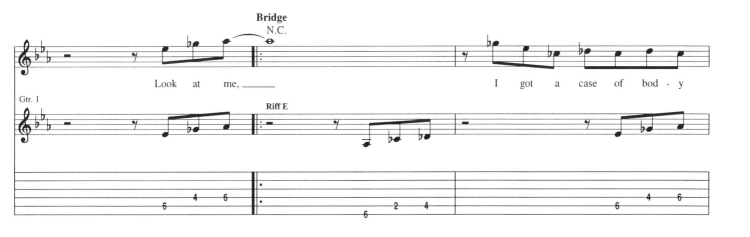

Bridge
N.C.

Look at me, _____ I got a case of bod-y

Gtr. 1   **Riff E**

lan-guage. ____ | 1., 2., 3. | | 4. |

Look at me, _ of bod-y

End Riff E

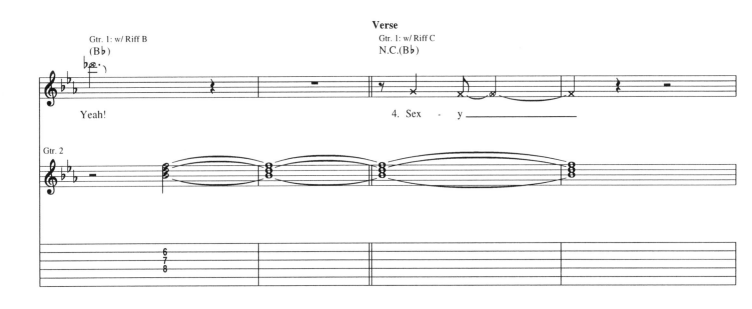

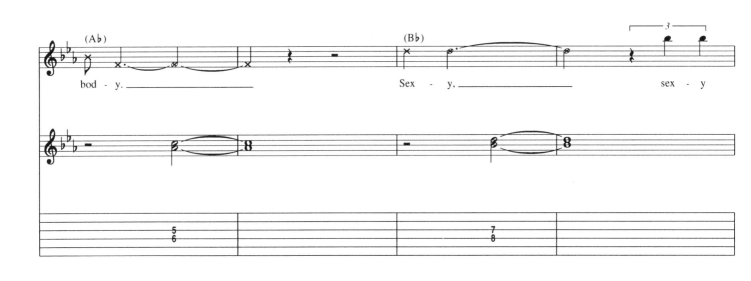

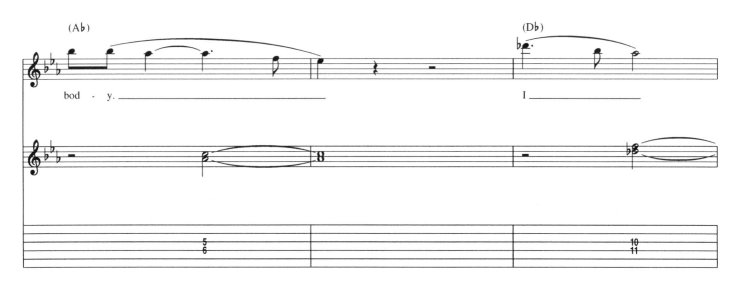

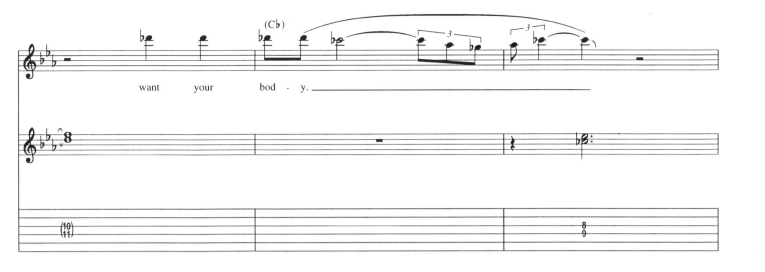

want your bod - y. _____

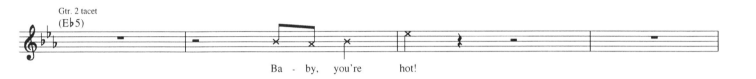

Gtr. 2 tacet
(E♭5)

Ba - by, you're hot!

Gtr. 1: w/ Riff A, 2 times
Gtr. 1: w/ Riff B
(B♭)

Bod - y

Outro   *Play 4 Times and Fade*
Gtr. 1: w/ Riff B, 2 times
Gtr. 3: w/ Fill 1, 2nd, 3rd & 4th times   Gtr. 3: w/ Fill 1, 4th time
N.C.(B♭)

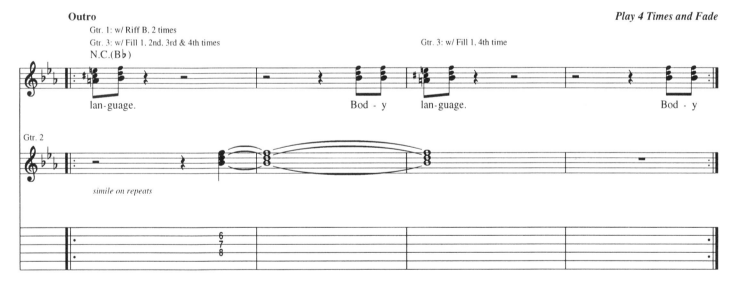

lan-guage.   Bod - y   lan-guage.   Bod - y

Gtr. 2

simile on repeats

Fill 1
Gtr. 3 (dist.)

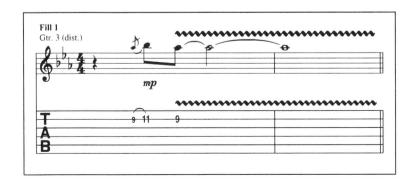

mp

Save Me

Words and Music by Brian May

years be - lie, __ we lived __ a lie. __ I'll love __ you __ 'til I die. __

End Rhy. Fig. 2

(cont. in slash)

Chorus
(drums enter)

Rhy. Fig. 3
Gtr. 2

Save me, save me, save me, __ I can't face this life __ a -

Gtr. 3
(elec.)

mf w/ dist.

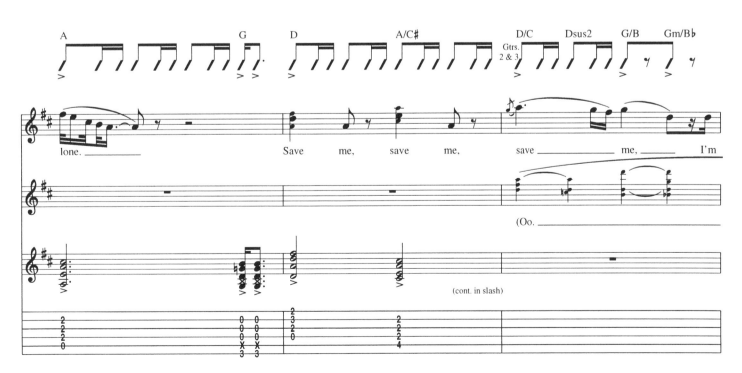

Gtrs.
2 & 3

lone. __ Save me, save me, save __ me, __ I'm

(Oo. __

(cont. in slash)

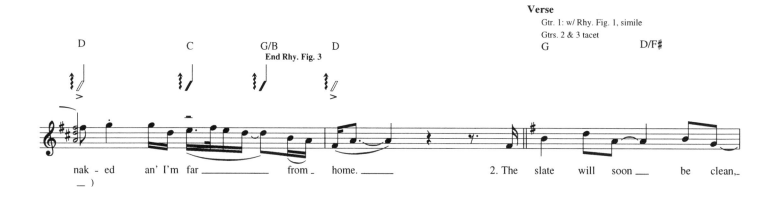

nak - ed an' I'm far _____ from _ home. _____ 2. The slate will soon _ be clean,_
_)

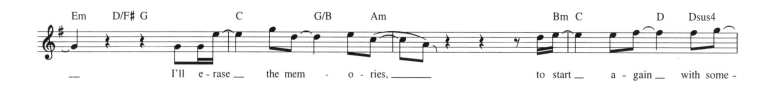

_ I'll e - rase _ the mem - o - ries, _____ to start _ a - gain _ with some -

- bod - y new. _ Was it all _ wast - ed, all that love? _ I hang my head _____ and I

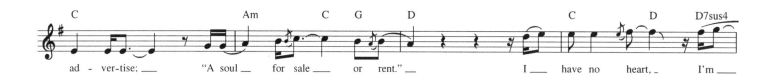

ad - ver - tise; _ "A soul _ for sale _ or rent." _ I _ have no heart,_ I'm _

_ cold _ in - side, _ I have _ no _ real in - tent. _____

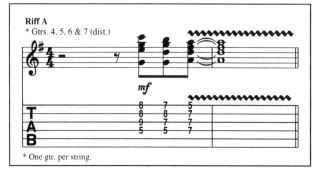

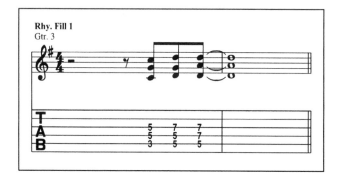

Chorus

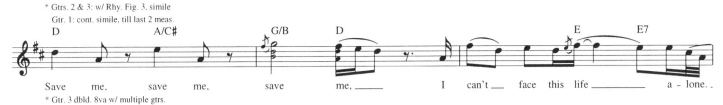

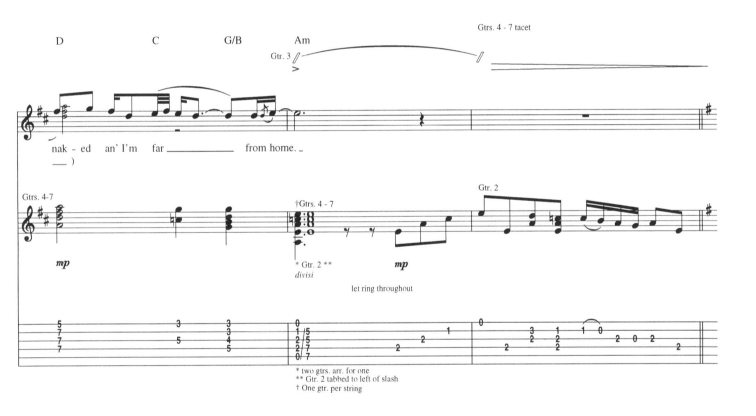

* two gtrs. arr. for one
** Gtr. 2 tabbed to left of slash
† One gtr. per string

Interlude

Outro

Don't Stop Me Now

Words and Music by Freddie Mercury

burn - in' through _ the _ sky, _ yeah, _ two hun - dred de - grees, _ that's why they

call me Mis - ter Fah - ren - heit. _____ I'm trav - 'ling at the speed of light, _

_____ I wan - na make a su - per - son - ic man out of you. _____

End Rhy. Fig. 3

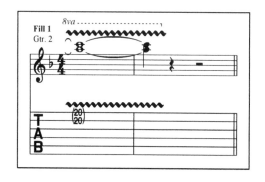

Verse

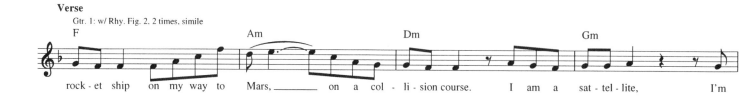

rock-et ship on my way to Mars, ___ on a col-li-sion course. I am a sat-tel-lite, I'm

out of con-trol. ___ I'm a sex ma-chine read-y to re-load, like an at-om bomb a-bout to

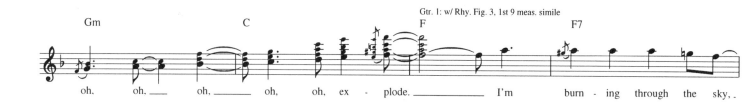

oh, oh, ___ oh, ___ oh, oh, ex-plode. ___ I'm burn-ing through the sky, __

___ yeah, ___ two hun-dred de-grees, __ that's why they call me Mis-ter Fah-ren-heit. ___ I'm

trav-'ling at the speed of light, ___ I wan-na make a su-per-son-ic wom-an of you. ___

Bridge

Hey, hey, _ hey! ___

Don't stop me, don't stop me, don't stop me. Don't stop me, don't stop me, oo,

I ___ like ___ it, ___ have a good time, good time. ___ Oh!

oo, oo. ___ Don't stop me, don't stop me. Al-right. ___ Don't stop me, don't stop me. Oh! ___

110

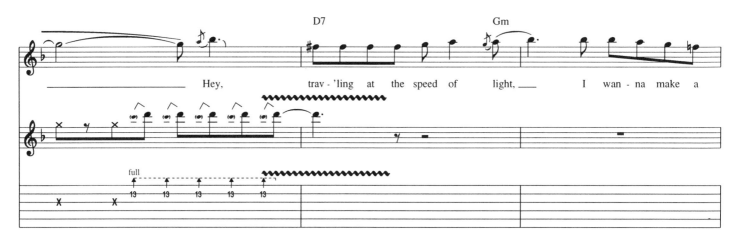

Hey, trav-'ling at the speed of light,____ I wan-na make a

D.S. al Coda

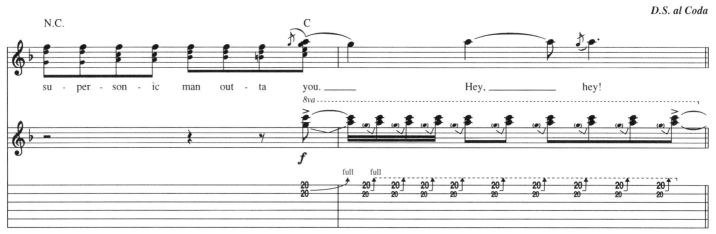

su-per-son-ic man out-ta you.____ Hey,____ hey!

$\oplus$ *Coda*

Slower ♩ = 96

Outro

Gtr. 1: w/ Rhy. Fig. 1, simile, till end

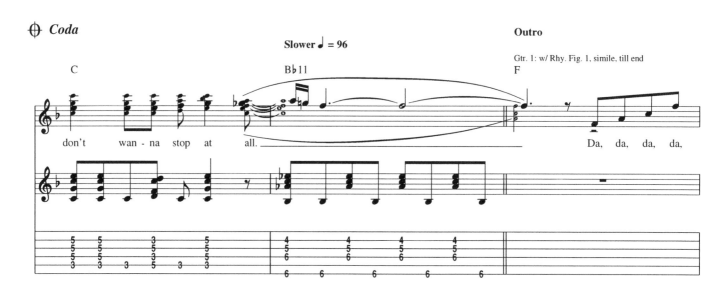

don't wan-na stop at all.____ Da, da, da, da,

da,____ da, da, da.____ Ha, da, da, ha,____ ha, ha.____ Ha, da,

Begin Fade

Fade Out

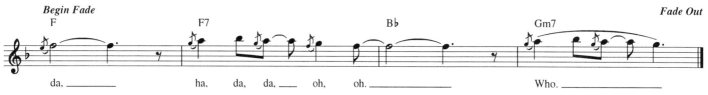

da,____ ha, da, da,____ oh, oh. Who.____

Good Old-Fashioned Lover Boy

Words and Music by Freddie Mercury

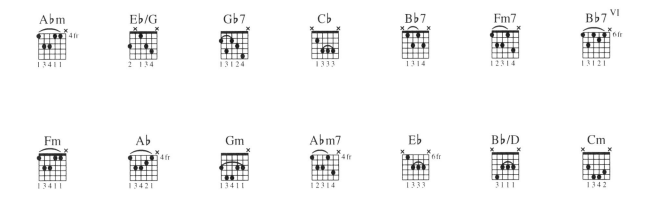

* Piano arr. for gtr.

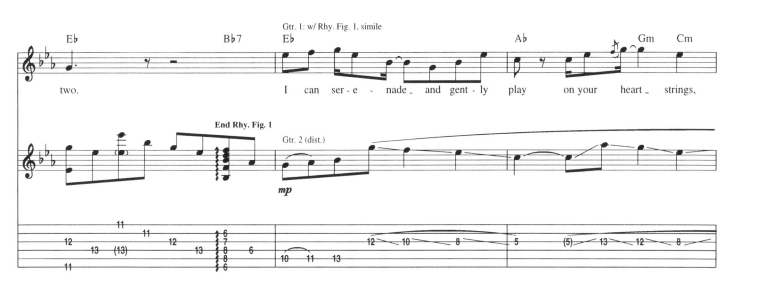

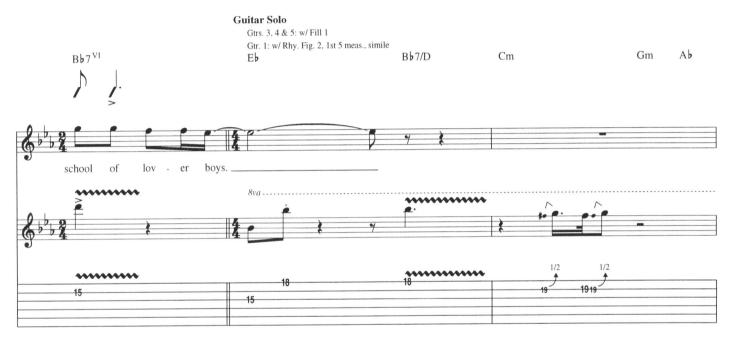

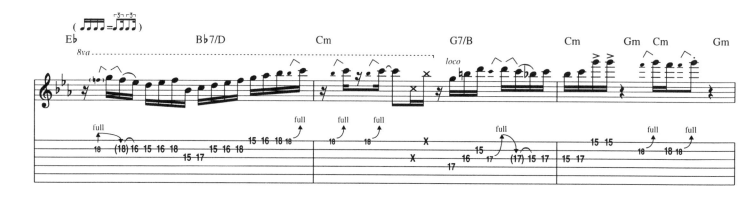

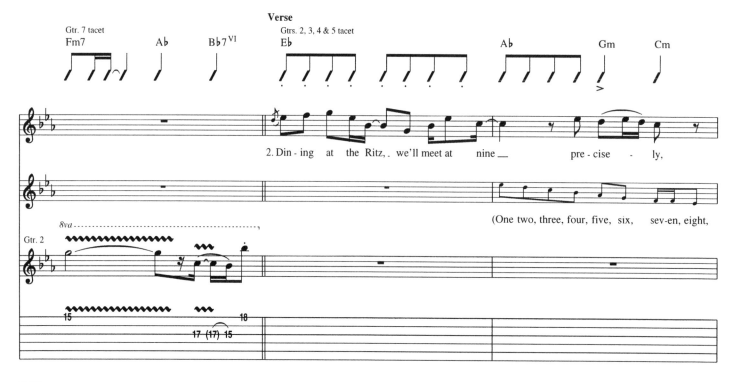

I Want to Break Free

Words and Music by John Deacon

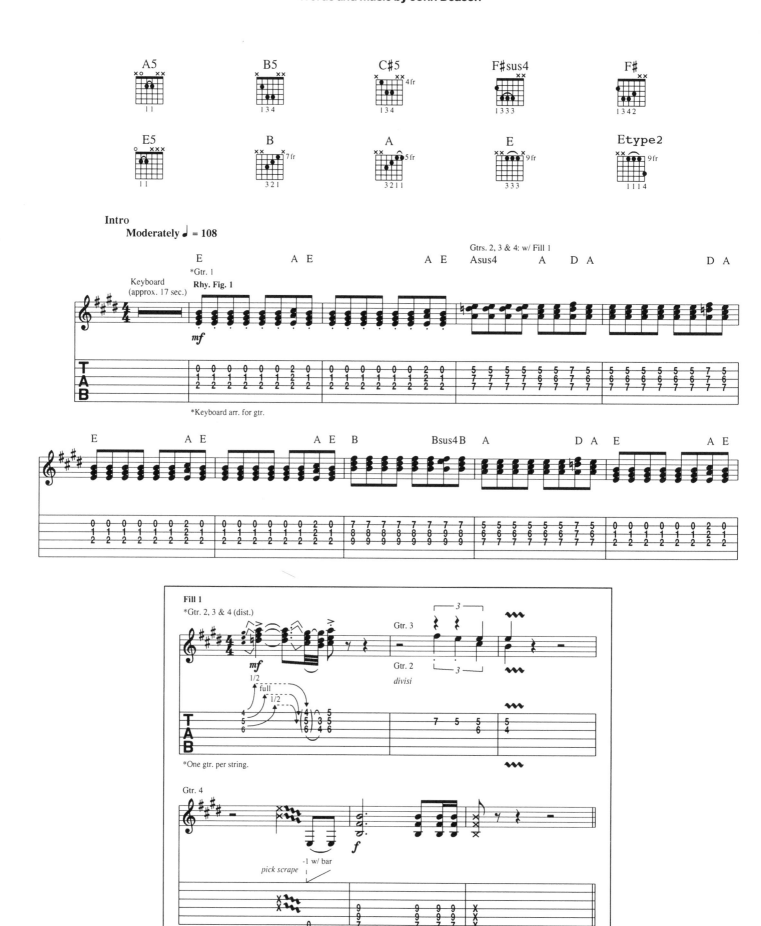

Chorus

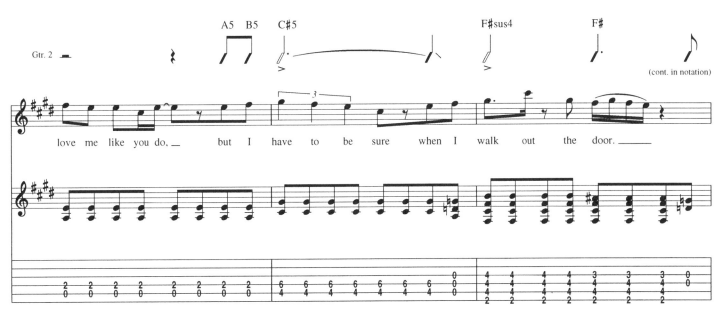

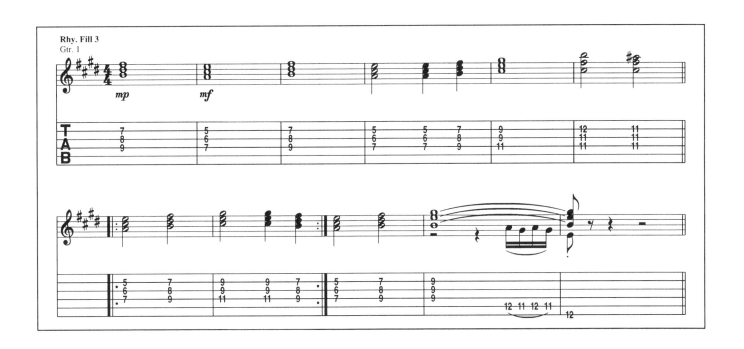

Oh, how I want to be free, ba - by,   oh, how I want to be free. _____   Oh,—

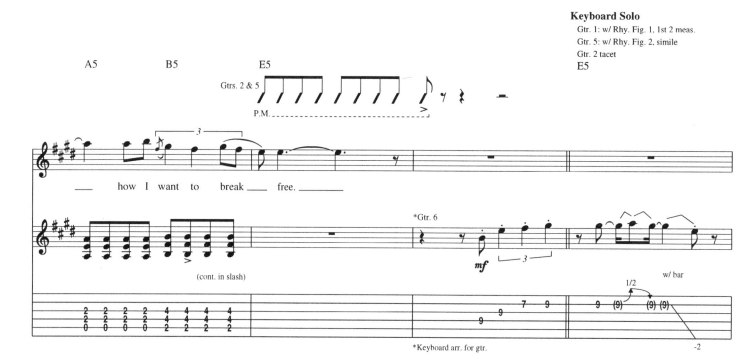

Keyboard Solo
Gtr. 1: w/ Rhy. Fig. 1, 1st 2 meas.
Gtr. 5: w/ Rhy. Fig. 2, simile
Gtr. 2 tacet

_____ how I want to break _____ free. _____

*Keyboard arr. for gtr.

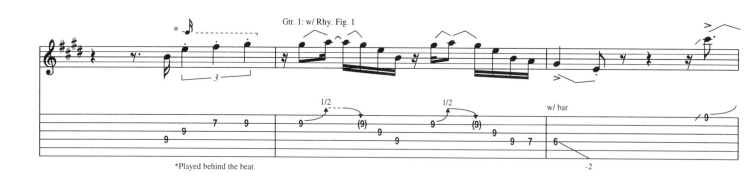

*Played behind the beat.

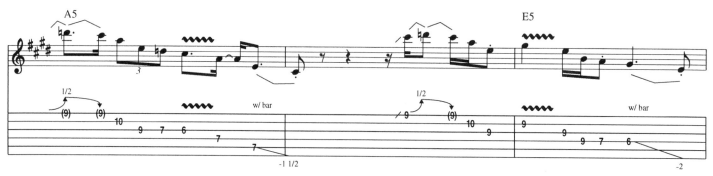

Coda

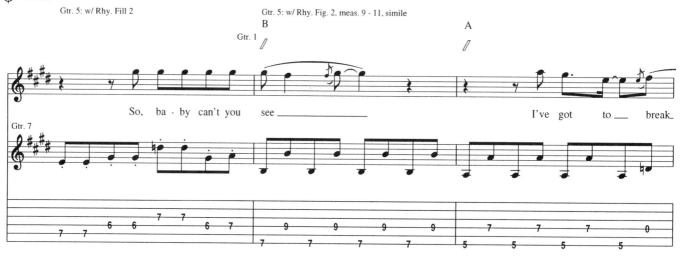

Outro

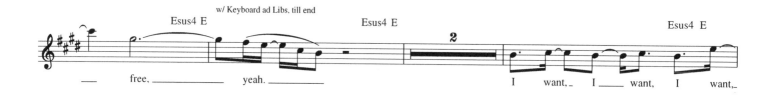

126

Guitar Notation Legend

Guitar Music can be notated three different ways: on a *musical staff*, in *tablature*, and in *rhythm slashes*.

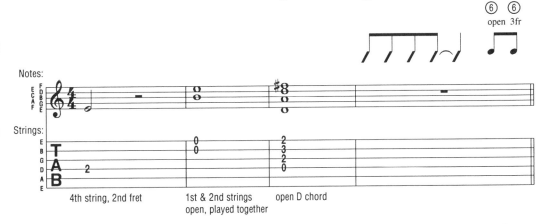

RHYTHM SLASHES are written above the staff. Strum chords in the rhythm indicated. Use the chord diagrams found at the top of the first page of the transcription for the appropriate chord voicings. Round noteheads indicate single notes.

THE MUSICAL STAFF shows pitches and rhythms and is divided by bar lines into measures. Pitches are named after the first seven letters of the alphabet.

TABLATURE graphically represents the guitar fingerboard. Each horizontal line represents a a string, and each number represents a fret.

Definitions for Special Guitar Notation

HALF-STEP BEND: Strike the note and bend up 1/2 step.

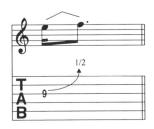

WHOLE-STEP BEND: Strike the note and bend up one step.

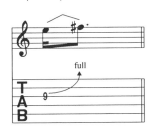

GRACE NOTE BEND: Strike the note and bend up as indicated. The first note does not take up any time.

SLIGHT (MICROTONE) BEND: Strike the note and bend up 1/4 step.

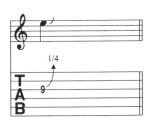

BEND AND RELEASE: Strike the note and bend up as indicated, then release back to the original note. Only the first note is struck.

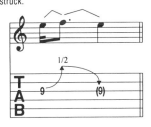

PRE-BEND: Bend the note as indicated, then strike it.

PRE-BEND AND RELEASE: Bend the note as indicated. Strike it and release the bend back to the original note.

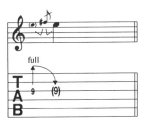

UNISON BEND: Strike the two notes simultaneously and bend the lower note up to the pitch of the higher.

VIBRATO: The string is vibrated by rapidly bending and releasing the note with the fretting hand.

WIDE VIBRATO: The pitch is varied to a greater degree by vibrating with the fretting hand.

HAMMER-ON: Strike the first (lower) note with one finger, then sound the higher note (on the same string) with another finger by fretting it without picking.

PULL-OFF: Place both fingers on the notes to be sounded. Strike the first note and without picking, pull the finger off to sound the second (lower) note.

LEGATO SLIDE: Strike the first note and then slide the same fret-hand finger up or down to the second note. The second note is not struck.

SHIFT SLIDE: Same as legato slide, except the second note is struck.

TRILL: Very rapidly alternate between the notes indicated by continuously hammering on and pulling off.

TAPPING: Hammer ("tap") the fret indicated with the pick-hand index or middle finger and pull off to the note fretted by the fret hand.

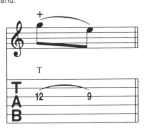

127

NATURAL HARMONIC: Strike the note while the fret-hand lightly touches the string directly over the fret indicated.

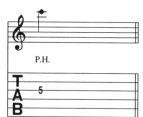

PINCH HARMONIC: The note is fretted normally and a harmonic is produced by adding the edge of the thumb or the tip of the index finger of the pick hand to the normal pick attack.

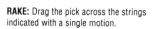

HARP HARMONIC: The note is fretted normally and a harmonic is produced by gently resting the pick hand's index finger directly above the indicated fret (in parentheses) while the pick hand's thumb or pick assists by plucking the appropriate string.

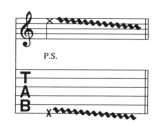

PICK SCRAPE: The edge of the pick is rubbed down (or up) the string, producing a scratchy sound.

MUFFLED STRINGS: A percussive sound is produced by laying the fret hand across the string(s) without depressing, and striking them with the pick hand.

PALM MUTING: The note is partially muted by the pick hand lightly touching the string(s) just before the bridge.

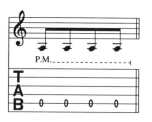

RAKE: Drag the pick across the strings indicated with a single motion.

TREMOLO PICKING: The note is picked as rapidly and continuously as possible.

ARPEGGIATE: Play the notes of the chord indicated by quickly rolling them from bottom to top.

VIBRATO BAR DIVE AND RETURN: The pitch of the note or chord is dropped a specified number of steps (in rhythm) then returned to the original pitch.

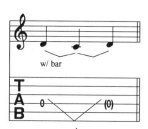

VIBRATO BAR SCOOP: Depress the bar just before striking the note, then quickly release the bar.

VIBRATO BAR DIP: Strike the note and then immediately drop a specified number of steps, then release back to the original pitch.

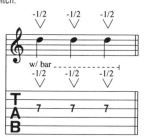

Additional Musical Definitions

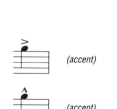

(accent) • Accentuate note (play it louder)

(accent) • Accentuate note with great intensity

(staccato) • Play the note short

⊓ • Downstroke

∨ • Upstroke

D.S. al Coda • Go back to the sign (𝄋), then play until the measure marked "***To Coda***," then skip to the section labelled "***Coda***."

D.S. al Fine • Go back to the beginning of the song and play until the measure marked "***Fine***" (end).

Rhy. Fig. • Label used to recall a recurring accompaniment pattern (usually chordal).

Riff • Label used to recall composed, melodic lines (usually single notes) which recur.

Fill • Label used to identify a brief melodic figure which is to be inserted into the arrangement.

Rhy. Fill • A chordal version of a Fill.

tacet • Instrument is silent (drops out).

• Repeat measures between signs.

• When a repeated section has different endings, play the first ending only the first time and the second ending only the

NOTE: Tablature numbers in parentheses mean:
1. The note is being sustained over a system (note in standard notation is tied), or
2. The note is sustained, but a new articulation (such as a hammer-on, pull-off, slide or vibrato begins, or
3. The note is a barely audible "ghost" note (note in standard notation is also in parentheses).